Private Business ... Public Battleground

Private Business ... Public Battleground

The case for twenty-first century stakeholder companies

John Egan and Des Wilson

(with Susan Cunnington King)

with introductions by

Mark Goyder (Tomorrow's Company),
David Grayson (Business in the Community)
and Jonathon Porritt (Forum for the Future)

palgrave

First published 2002 by
PALGRAVE
Houndmills, Basingstoke, Hampshire RG21 6XS and
175 Fifth Avenue, New York, N.Y. 10010
Companies and representatives throughout the world

PALGRAVE is the global academic imprint of
St. Martin's Press LLC Scholarly and Reference Division and
Palgrave Publishers Ltd (formerly Macmillan Press Ltd).

ISBN 0–333–92939–X

This book is printed on paper suitable for recycling and made from fully managed and sustained forest sources.

Cataloguing-in-publication data

A catalogue record for this book is available from the British Library.

A catalogue record for this book is available from the Library of Congress

10 9 8 7 6 5 4 3 2 1
11 10 09 08 07 06 05 04 03 02

Editing and origination by
Curran Publishing Services, Norwich, Norfolk

Printed in Great Britain by
Creative Print & Design (Ebbw Vale), Wales

CONTENTS

Authors' Note

There is a gap in time between the writing of a book and its publication. When we wrote this book the Western world – at least – was blessed with peace and prosperity. The aviation industry we both worked in for over five years was planning for growth. But just as we were delivering the manuscript that world was blown apart by terrorist action in New York and Washington, precipitating international responses and tensions with an outcome that we even now cannot predict. Economies were in turmoil and the aviation industry, in particular, virtually fell apart, with airlines facing bankruptcy, employees being made redundant, passengers' options being reduced. It seemed unlikely a world recession could be avoided.

You will now know what we could not know: what actually has happened over the past three or four months. We can only hope that the world community's determination to stamp out terrorism is achieving results, and that the hopes we had at the turn of the Millennium that we can enjoy even more peace and prosperity in the twenty-first century are returning.

What we do know is that more than ever the world will need the wealth and employment that industry can generate, that it will need the innovation that can make lives better and longer, and that it will need the global reach of business to be balanced by a greater contribution to tackling the imbalances of wealth and justice that currently exist. Rather than being outdated by events, we believe the fundamental message of this book has been reinforced by recent experience, namely that business and industry cannot exist in isolation from the world around it. We are all citizens – of our cities, our countries, our world – and all have a stake in them, just as they have a stake in our companies, our success and how we achieve it. This book is about people working together; there has never been a time when that call is more relevant.

John Egan and Des Wilson

Acknowledgements

Our thanks to Mike Hodgkinson and colleagues at BAA for their permission to draw so heavily on our experiences with the company, and for their assistance generally.

Also to Chris Hoare, the company's first Community Relations Director, for his input, and to Andrew Currie, his successor, who has been immensely helpful.

Susan Cunnington King made an indispensable contribution and we are grateful to David Grayson for his advice, his introductory contribution, and for access to his recent book, co-authored with Adrian Hodges, *Everybody's Business: Managing Opportunities and Risks in Today's Global Society* (Dorling Kindersley and the *Financial Times*).

Special thanks to John Underwood for allowing us to draw from, and quote extensively from his book, *The Will to Win: John Egan and Jaguar*, published by W.H. Allen in 1989, and to Mark Goyder and Jonathon Porritt for their contributions to the introductory section. Along with John Elkington's SustainAbility, theirs are essential organisations and their work in their respective areas is world-renowned.

Other publications that influenced our thinking and therefore this book, and some from which we quote directly are: *The Lead Scandal* by Des Wilson (Heinemann, 1993), *The Living Company* by Arie de Geus (HBS Press, 1996), *Cannibals with Forks* by John Elkington (Capstone, 1997) and *The Chrysalis Economy* by John Elkington (Capstone and John Wiley, 2001), *Corporate Citizenship* by McIntosh, Lepziger, Jones and Coleman (FT Pitman, 1998), *Built to Last* by James C. Collins and Jerry I. Porras (Harper Business, 1994), *No Logo* by Naomi Klein (Flamingo, 2000), and *Built to Last* (published by SustainAbility Ltd and the UN Environment Programme).

Foreword
The Right Thing

Mike Hodgkinson, Chief Executive, BAA plc

My former colleagues John Egan and Des Wilson are right to stress that BAA would not claim to have yet become the perfect stakeholder company. In any case perfection belongs to a black and white world and the one we occupy is more complicated than that, not least because whatever pleases one stakeholder can displease another. For instance, growth in the number of passengers at a particular airport will please our City stakeholders because it means increased revenue, but is not such good news for our neighbours, over whose heads the additional planes will fly. There will always be a conflict between, on the one hand, the economic and, indeed, social imperatives to achieve continual growth and, on the other, the constraints imposed by the need to do so sustainably. That is why Egan and Wilson are right to stress that what matters is not that a company is perfect but that – at a time when we are seeking to understand the full meaning of, and routes to stakeholderism, let alone sustainability – it genuinely tries to do all it can to address and balance the interests of all it affects. That is what I believe we in BAA are trying to do. We are enthusiastic participants in what the authors call the twenty-first century revolution.

This book is published shortly after we were given permission to build a fifth terminal (T5) at Heathrow and at the outset of a major debate about how the UK confronts the challenge of growth in aviation after the crisis following 11 September 2000 is ended as we all hope it will be. I hope one of the book's benefits will be a greater knowledge of how much BAA has done to meet its social obligations, as well as an understanding of those environmental and other sustainability issues that are beyond its ability to determine but that it is trying to influence.

But the book is not just about BAA. It draws on our company to identify who stakeholders are or could be, and to describe some of the issues that have to be addressed. It shows how BAA set out in the mid-1990s on a journey that can never end … to do 'the right thing'. But it also makes the case for corporate citizenship generally, shows how business and industry are increasingly coming to understand not only that there is a moral or social case for the stakeholder approach but also that it is plain and simple 'good business'. It shows how bankrupt is the debate between shareholder and stakeholder value.

Egan taught BAA how to put the customer first, and the company reaped the rewards. Wilson taught it how to relate better to the wider world, and especially to its neighbours, and the company is undoubtedly benefiting from that too. But for me what has been exciting has been to see how my colleagues at every level of BAA are embracing these principles and making them their own. The authors are also right to stress in this book that corporate citizenship must be the cause of everyone in a company, from the boardroom to the shop floor. Unless there is unity of purpose, it simply won't work.

There are many reasons why the stakeholder approach is the only realistic and practical one for companies like BAA, acting (as the authors describe it) at the interface between private commerce and the public interest. But there is one special reason, and that is the pride it gives everyone in the places where they spend so many hours of their lives. To hear one's colleagues proudly proclaim 'this is a good company' is justification enough.

As the book argues, we are living in a fast-changing world. You have only to consider the dramatic change that has occurred in the aviation industry between the writing of the book and today. One feature of that change is greater environmental awareness and greater pressure on companies to share responsibility with the community for building a fair and just society. There will come a day when it will seem extraordinary that there were ever companies that did not embrace corporate citizenship. But until quite recently the sceptics were in the majority, and there are still too many. If our experiences and those of other companies referred to in this book, our and their successes and failures, but above all our determination to do better, help others to set out on a similar path or to reinforce their efforts to what the authors describe as 'the right thing', then this book is more than worthwhile.

Introduction
Setting the Scene

Connected Economy – Disjointed Society
What Can We Hope for from Global Capitalism?

Mark Goyder

Behind the debate about how far business and industry have yet to go to meet wider environmental and social concerns is an even wider world-wide debate about the impacts of global capitalism.

The author of this introduction is Director of the Centre for Tomorrow's Company.

Views of the future of global capitalism vary. The gloomy view holds global capitalism responsible for destroying employment, impoverishing the self-sufficient, destroying biodiversity, undermining local control, crushing indigenous culture and diversity, increasing inequality, imposing a consumerism culture driven by advertising, and separating investors from any sense of responsibility for their investment.

For example, David Korten, who published *When Corporations Rule The World* in 1995, defines the crisis in terms of deepening poverty, social disintegration and environmental destruction. The typical pattern of globalised capitalist growth, says Korten, looks like this:

1. Increased depletion of natural resources.
2. Shifting activities from the social (non-money) economy to the money economy, thus increasing the dependence of the working classes on money.
3. Shifting control of agricultural lands, forests and fisheries from those engaged in creating subsistence livelihoods to property owners investing for profit.

A very similar critique was made in a Reith Lecture by Vandana Shiva.

> I was in Warangal, Andrha Pradesh, where farmers have ... been
> committing suicide. Farmers who traditionally grew pulses and
> millets and paddy have been lured by seed companies to buy hybrid
> cotton seeds referred to by the seed merchants as 'white gold', which
> were supposed to make them millionaires. Instead they became
> paupers.
>
>   Their native seeds have been displaced with new hybrids which
> cannot be saved and need to be purchased every year at high cost.
> Hybrids are also very vulnerable to pest attacks. Spending on pesti-
> cides in Warangal has shot up 2000 per cent from $ 2.5 million in the
> 1980s to $ 50 million in 1997. Now farmers are consuming the same
> pesticides as a way of killing themselves so that they can escape
> permanently from unpayable debt.

Packaging regulations represent another damaging intervention by global
capitalism. Vandana Shiva reports:

> In August 1998, small-scale local processing of edible oil was
> banned in India through a 'packaging order' which made sale of
> open oil illegal and required all oil to be packaged in plastic or
> aluminium. This shut down tiny ... mills. It destroyed the market for
> our diverse oilseeds – mustard, linseed, sesame, groundnut, coconut.

The take-over of the edible oil industry has affected 10 million livelihoods.
The take-over of flour or 'atta' by packaged, branded flour will cost 100
million livelihoods. And these millions are being pushed into new poverty.
      Then there is the impact of new global intellectual property rules. Shiva
concludes:

> The waste of the rich is being dumped on the poor. The wealth of the
> poor is being violently appropriated through new and clever means
> like patents on biodiversity and indigenous knowledge.
>
>   Patents and intellectual property rights are supposed to be
> granted for novel inventions. But patents are being claimed for rice
> varieties such as the basmati for which my valley – where I was born
> – is famous....

Every aspect of the innovation embodied in our indigenous food and medicinal systems is now being pirated and patented. The knowledge of the poor is being converted into the property of global corporations, creating a situation where the poor will have to pay for the seeds and medicines they have evolved and have used to meet their own needs for nutrition and health care.

Such false claims to creation are now the global norm, with the Trade Related Intellectual Property Rights Agreement of the World Trade Organisation forcing countries to introduce regimes that allow patenting of life forms and indigenous knowledge.

By this analysis, global capitalism redistributes from poor to rich. It may boost the GDP of a country which embraces it, but on all the indicators of human well-being it has made things worse. Certainly companies are powerful agents of change, but they are willing contributors to a change process that is dehumanising, destabilising and environmentally degrading.

I draw a distinction between the impact of global capitalism on the underdeveloped world and its impact on a relatively rich country like the UK. It is not the job of business to keep subsidising unprofitable activity. It is the responsibility of business to take harsh decisions in a sensitive way, and to communicate them well. I guess the difference is that we are already paid-up members of the global economy. We know what we are letting ourselves in for, and as consumers we all say we want the benefits of lower prices and higher product performance. You cannot say that about the farmers of Andrha Pradesh.

What about the new economy? Here too there is plenty for the pessimists to brood on. The knowledge economy which has been developing over the last 15 years deepens the divide between rich and poor. Two hundred and fifty years ago the difference in income per head between the richest and poorest nations in the world was five to one. Today it is 400 to one. According to the UN, inequality between rich and poor has doubled in 15 years. There was fresh evidence of a growing gulf between rich and poor in the UK in the official statistics on inequality published in 2001. At the start of the 1970s the incomes of the richest 10 per cent were three times higher than those of the poorest. By the end of the 1990s they were four times higher.

It is also easy to see the forces in capitalism which attack diversity. We are now seeing the convergence of all the different media: TV, computing, telephones. We are seeing the creation of ever larger commercial giants who will control the provision of content.

Then there are the issues of access. For the connected few, the new world of communications is full of promise. But what of those without fast access?

According to the US Commerce Department, rich Americans are 20 times more likely to have Internet access than poor ones.

So here we have a world in which the WTO and the IMF provide the only rulebook, and Wall Street the only values. Globalisation, according to the gloomy view, means monoculture and dispossession.

Let me now turn to some more encouraging views of global capitalism. The positive view sees business as an agent of social progress. It is business that delivers innovation, and solves pressing global problems by devising new solutions. Business can only secure the full benefits of knowledge by building high-quality relationships which rely on trust. Business cannot thrive except in a sustainable planet and a stable world. Business is in turn made up of individual people who have a sense of responsibility towards the planet and communities within it.

The knowledge economy remains a relationships economy.

Many will have heard BP Chairman Sir John Browne, who also delivered a Reith lecture. Sir John's thesis could be summarised thus:

1. Business is not in opposition to sustainable development; it is in fact essential for delivering it.
2. Few businesses are short-term; they want to do business again and again, over decades.
3. Business needs a sustainable planet and society for its own survival.
4. Business is the driver of innovation; changes in technology and in the way the economy works are giving the means to deliver genuine progress. (Browne's examples included the commitment to reduce the emission of greenhouse gases by 10 per cent from the 1990 benchmark, and he observed that in the last year his company had achieved a reduction of 4 per cent.)
5. If you want problems solved effectively and fast, come to business. (Browne cited Shell's emission-free gas-fired power station now planned for Norway, and work that will soon lead to the development of emission-free cars.)
6. What keeps business honest is the combined influence of employees,

shareholders, the public and government; there is now a revolution in reporting and transparency which keeps business accountable in a holistic way.

7. People who work in business care about the planet; this helps to shape what business does.

8. Civil society can also influence business, and this will happen through a process of transparency; companies will report on their social and environmental impacts, and have targets.

Sir John talked about the connected economy as an opportunity.

This optimistic view is indeed supported by most prophets of the new economy. The world-wide web, in their view, is a tool that enables individuals to be treated more sensitively according to their individual needs and preferences. The web offers a space where customers and stakeholders develop conversations with companies.

In exploring its potential benefits I came across a fascinating book by David Siegel called *Futurize Your Enterprise: Business Strategy in the Age of the E-Customer*. Siegel argues that new organisations are made possible by the web because it facilitates new kinds of conversations. 'Perhaps the biggest difference between the way we do business today and the way we will do business tomorrow is that we will all become better listeners.'

Siegel argues that the globally interconnected economy is perfectly designed for inclusivity. It treats people as individuals; it gives them a voice; it breaks through the communication bottleneck where you are speaking to the official voice of the company. It equips human beings to be more human in their pursuit of economic goals.

This is true for customers. And it could also be true for other stakeholders.

In his lecture Sir John Browne described the process by which BP is 'kept honest' by the interlocking pressures applied by its staff, its shareholders, its public and governments around the world. He explained that social and environmental goals have become part of the measurement system. If you look at a recent annual review by BP Amoco, it describes itself as 'the first fully integrated report BP Amoco has produced: recording our financial, social and environmental performance, and linking our printed and on-line reports to create a living website'. The aim, the company explains, is to offer detailed and updated access throughout the year on how the group works and how it achieves its performance. One of the features of the website is an opportunity to put questions directly to the CEO.

And what of the needs of society? There are optimists and pessimists. What I find lacking among the pessimists is the beginnings of a solution. The obvious synthesis between the two is to accept much of the diagnosis of the pessimists, but to accept from the optimists the argument that business does provide the source of many of the solutions. To hammer out a new kind of synthesis we will need different approaches to governance and to dialogue. New governance and new dialogue are essential, and several forces are now combining to make them possible. I will mention four:

- the rise of the NGO
- the emergence of conversation friendly technology
- new pressures on governance and reporting
- new opportunities for innovation in investment.

In 1900 there were only 20 international governmental organisations (IGOs) and 180 international non-governmental organisations (NGOs). There are now over 300 IGOs and 5000 NGOs. There is no shortage of organisations with whom to hold the dialogue. The issue now is how to make the dialogue meaningful.

With the new technology, it becomes possible for companies to conduct thousands of simultaneous conversations with their stakeholders. In the past there was just one occasion a year when the board of a major company might come face to face with its critics: the AGM. But that is an extreme safety valve. The criticisms of global companies that I have described earlier should now be channelled directly to the board members and managers responsible. Information and communications technology could begin to bring the human consequences of a company's actions right into the head office itself. This would be done in pictures as well as words. Companies cannot be expected to roll over and surrender all their competitive advantage, but every company can now be forced to say how its actions can be squared with its values, and with its professed desire to be a good citizen. The conversation might not be only with the public affairs department. Stakeholders can reach other employees around the company who care about its impact and its values. It is time to stop treating the company like a monolith. Start treating it like the 'quasi-democracy' to which Sir John Browne refers.

Just as the e-commerce agenda is helping companies talk more sensitively to their customers, so it will help business to practise the art of conversation with all its stakeholders. Meanwhile, the increasingly influential NGOs and stakeholder conversations will stimulate companies to measure and report on their impacts in areas previously not covered. In the next few years, the critical indicators of performance for a multinational food or energy company will be the impact its actions have on inequality and social distribution as well as biodiversity.

Here is where UK company law is going to help. In the UK there are now new company law proposals for a mandatory operating and financial review covering a company's purpose, strategy and principal drivers of performance. As part of the same review, large companies will also be required to set out, where material, an account of their key relationships with employees, customers, suppliers and others on whom the success of the business depends. The requirement goes on to mention environmental policies and performance, as well as community, social and reputational issues.

The key point is that these requirements will not come in a separate 'glossy' to keep the NGOs happy. They will be required as part of the central account to shareholders on how the company has performed and how it intends to do business. The social and ethical agenda is mainstream, because it affects long-term performance.

Which brings us to shareholders. Perhaps some business people are human, say the cynics. The problem is that they are not allowed to act humanely by the shareholders, who are interested only in their quarterly return and care neither for the long-term performance, nor the human impacts. And, David Korten would doubtless add, the same is true of the IMF and the World Bank.

Here, it seems to me, is where the most important work is to be done in taking the potential provided by the new technology and applying it in a way which enriches the diversity of our economy.

John Browne's argument about BP – that it is a community of individual people who all have their own concerns about the planet and what the company might be doing to it – could equally well be applied to Merrill Lynch or Schroders or Gartmore and the collective funds which they invest on our behalf. These investment managers are intermediaries who represent individual savers and investors who – just like the employees of BP – all have their own concerns about the planet and what the companies in which they are investing might be doing to it.

It is no coincidence that the quantity of money under ethical management is now growing as individual investors exercise their market power. Since 1998 the amount invested in UK ethical trusts has jumped from £ 1.7 billion to £ 2.8 billion, a gain of 64 per cent. Ethical funds too are becoming more sophisticated. In time there will be funds which reward well-led companies. No longer will savers be fobbed off by glib advisers telling them they must trade off ethical concerns for financial returns.

'Markets are conversations'. Capital markets too are conversations. At present the level of conversation is immature, but as technology makes individual citizens of us all, the opportunity will soon exist to obtain our long-terms returns from companies on an altogether more sustainable basis. Changing the climate so that this becomes possible is, as I see it, one of the key tasks for Tomorrow's Company in the years ahead.

Technology, the rise of the NGO, a new agenda for governance, and the rise of a more engaged form of ethical investment are converging to give us a moment of real opportunity.

We need to accept much of the cynics' diagnosis of the past, and much of the optimists' view of the power business has as an agent for change. In particular, we need to remember that even before the new economy, business has been experiencing the death of deference – and this is not just about an abandonment of formal dress. Large companies can only do what people inside and around them will let them do. They are now on the bottom steps of an escalator of transparency, and for most of them it is a positive experience to move up that escalator. Technology now allows companies to customise their treatment of customers and other stakeholders. The same is possible for investors. Businesses will face the urgent need to transform themselves by starting to see all markets, including capital markets, as conversations.

Diversity could be the connected economy's gift to our disjointed society.

Business and the Community
Dangerous Distraction or Commercial Imperative?
David Grayson

Business in the Community has led the movement in the UK towards greater corporate citizenship and the author of this introduction, one of its directors, has been particularly effective in relating the social benefits to a business rationale.

The name 'Coke' is the second most recognised word in the world after 'okay'. Coca Cola is a global brand, aiming to be 'within an armchair of desire'. Yet despite its global reach, it faced a challenge to its track-record on diversity on its own doorstep: black American employees took a 'battle bus' around the US protesting against Coca Cola's treatment of African-American employees, culminating at the corporation's AGM in April 2000. The Coca Cola Chairman and CEO, Douglas Daft, has said he will tie his compensation to diversity goals and create an executive position to develop strategies for promoting minorities. Coke subsequently settled a lawsuit by current and former African-American employees accusing the soft-drink company of racial bias for $ 190 million.

Nike will allow university students to visit its suppliers' factories in order 'to demonstrate that they are not "sweatshops"'. Nike had previously declined to make public the names and locations of its factories. The company's move came after intense pressure by student groups in the US who wanted to make independent assessments of factory conditions. Nike says it wants to 'raise the bar' for the industry on access to factories. The company will pay for 10 student activists to visit a total of 41 plants. They will travel with representatives of Nike's auditing firm, Pricewaterhouse-Coopers. Nike sells about $ 160 million each year in products carrying university labels.

Isolated examples or part of a pattern? I believe that:

- All over the world, there are growing expectations of how businesses will run their own affairs – and how they will help to tackle societal problems.
- This in turn means that issues that were once considered soft for business – the environment, diversity, human rights, health and well-being, community – have become hard for business. Hard to ignore, hard to manage – and very hard on a business that gets them wrong.
- Paradoxically, though, managing these same issues successfully can be a source of competitive advantage.

All over the world, the expectations of the way that a business will behave are changing and becoming more demanding. This is both about how a company conducts its own affairs, and how it impacts on and is involved in wider society.

Consumers want products and services that are fit for the purpose and good value, but they are also saying in increasing numbers that they expect businesses to behave responsibly. In the first ever global consumer survey on corporate social responsibility, 25 000 consumers in 23 countries – developed and developing – on six continents were asked in late 1999 about the changing role of companies for the Millennium CSR Poll.

This found that in forming impressions of companies, people around the world focus on corporate citizenship ahead of either brand reputation or financial factors. Fully half the population in the countries surveyed are paying attention to the social behaviour of companies. One in five consumers reported either rewarding or punishing companies in the past year based on their perceived social performance, and almost as many said they have considered doing so. The poll asked:

People have different views on the role of large companies in society. In your view, should large companies ...
- make profit, pay taxes, provide jobs and obey all laws?
- do all this in ways that set higher ethical standards, going beyond what is required by law, and actively helping build a better society for all?
- operate somewhere between these two points of view?

The first position – essentially the Milton Friedman line – was supported by a third of people polled across the world, with a third taking the view that large companies should go beyond what is required by law and actively help to build a better society. The balance think that companies should operate somewhere between these two positions.

Employees want good remuneration and good prospects, but people increasingly also want to feel proud of the company they work for.

Increasingly motivation is based on values rather than cash. Historically, loyalty was basically bought. The employer offered gradual progression up the hierarchy, a decent salary and job security. In return, the employee offered unwavering loyalty and a hard day's work. Now, values determine loyalty. 'Every organisation needs values, but a lean organisation needs them even more,' GE's Jack Welch says.

For stars there is a choice. They work for companies that are in accord with their own value systems. If they don't want to work for a polluter they will not. After all, people want to hold their heads up when they are with their peers. They don't want an embarrassed silence when they announce whom they work for. 'These days we value a great mission and a great working lifestyle as much as a bigger desk and the prospect of promotion.' According to *Newsweek* (31 January 2000), socially responsible investing in the US has increased 82 per cent since 1997 and is now worth nearly $2 trillion. In the UK, MORI surveys show that even institutional investors and City analysts are beginning to see the significance of these issues.

Non-governmental organisations and campaigning pressure groups are increasingly influential; they are organising on an international basis; and more of them are targeting businesses.

Politicians and other opinion formers are asking business to form partnerships with them. In the words of British Prime Minister Tony Blair:

> The twenty-first century company will be different. Many of Britain's best-known companies are already redefining traditional perceptions of the role of the corporation. They are recognising that every customer is part of a community, and that social responsibility is not an optional extra.

In March 2000, the heads of government of the European Union in the final communique of their Lisbon summit said:

> The European Council makes a special appeal to companies' corporate sense of social responsibility regarding best practices on life-long learning, work organisation, equal opportunities, social exclusion and sustainable development.

For me, the most compelling arguments are about talent and brand and trust. In the global war for talent, businesses simply cannot afford to make it harder to attract and retain the most talented people because they don't feel the business shares their values and wider social concerns. In a global market-place where brand and corporate reputation is so crucial – where the intangibles represent such a large part of market capitalisation: 83 per cent for IBM; 96 per cent for Coca Cola; 97 per cent for Kelloggs – what business leader really wants to risk putting that investment in brand and reputation at risk, because of some dodgy business practice somewhere in its world-wide operations, or – frighteningly – somewhere in its global supply chain?

Put those ideas of talent and brand together, in the issue of trust. What is driving greater expectations of business around the world? In two words: globalisation and technology.

In the decade since the Berlin Wall came tumbling down, three billion consumers have joined the global market economy and we have seen a relentless process of liberalisation, privatisation and globalisation. This has driven and been driven by rapid advances in technology, especially in information and communications technologies. When CNN came of age in the Gulf War, it had 8 million viewers outside the US. Today that figure is 151 million. And in the CNN world, there are no hiding places!

We are now in a time of dramatic change. A single day's growth in the US economy today is equal to the entire year's worth in 1830. The world trade of a single day is as great as in the entire year of 1949. The equivalent of all the science done in 1960 happens in one day today. All of the foreign exchange dealings around the world in 1979 would be performed in a day today, as would all the telephone calls made around the world in 1984. In one day now, as many e-mails are sent around the world as in the whole of 1989.

A key factor in this speeding up is the Internet. Bill Gates says that the Internet changes everything. I think he may be under-estimating its significance! In 1996, there were 60 million regular users world-wide. At the beginning of 2000, there were 275 million. The latest estimate is that by the end of 2002, the figure will be 600 million. The Internet changes the way we work, find work (e.g.: Monster.com with 15 million hits every month to its global recruitment website), learn, socialise and shop. Now you can put your money where your mouse is!

It also has huge consequences for people who want a say in how business is run. People who feel the same about business behaviour can find each other around the world to swop information and tactics. Tiny hand-held cameras the size of a cigarette packet will produce broadcast-quality pictures which can be sent over the Internet. A *Business Week* article highlighted that already over 100 major US brands are the subject of 'hate sites' on the Internet. Every week, I get six to eight electronic newsletters from NGOs around the world, monitoring corporate behaviour on environmental and social issues. The wired world may prove to be trip-wired for business!

I personally come from a political tradition that is strongly pro-market, and believe that responsible business is a crucial force for human progress and happiness. I work with an organisation – Business in the Community (BITC) – that is led by our business membership and whose mission is to inspire, not to bludgeon: 'to inspire business to increase the quality and extent of its contribution to social and economic regeneration by making corporate social responsibility an essential part of business excellence'. I passionately believe that business needs to heed the calls for changes in the way that it operates.

Companies that get it 'wrong' run the risk of:

- consumer boycotts
- finding it harder to recruit talent
- finding their 'Trust Bank' depleted
- hostile neighbours: 'dangerous intruders' syndrome
- isolation as admired companies shy away from partnerships that imply 'guilt by association'
- hostile regulators and public authorities
- campaigners'/media spotlight.

All these lead to distraction for management, limits on the company's freedom of manoeuvre, and threats to long-term profitability. Conversely, we believe these issues offer opportunities for competitive advantage if managed effectively:

- an enhanced reputation among consumers
- finding it easier to attract, develop, retain and motivate talented people
- increased goodwill and a 'Trust Bank' credit
- welcome from local communities that want your presence as a 'neighbour of choice'
- easier networking as admired companies seek you out
- benefit of the doubt from media, regulators, campaigners when problems occur, as they undoubtedly will even in 'good' companies
- new insights and skills from more eclectic networking.

All these build trust with different stakeholders, and improve the organisation's capacity for networking and for innovation.

An increasing number of major companies are now making commitments to responsible business, to good corporate citizenship and to the triple bottom line. Leading-edge companies are publishing environmental and social reports and using these reports as the basis for proactive dialogue with stakeholders. We need to persuade many more companies to follow their example. We also need to operationalise these ideas by helping line-managers to understand what they can do practically, where the rubber hits the road.

For example, every company which is already committed to sustainable business practices should now ensure that their management training programmes incorporate these issues as an integral part of the programme.

This is why John Egan and Des Wilson's book is such an important contribution to the widening debate about sustainable business excellence.

Businesses that want sustainably to add value for their owners now best achieve that by minimising the negative impacts and maximising the positive impacts that they have on society. This is the best guarantee of the continuation and expansion of open markets around the world, and thus the best way to ensure that responsible business continues to enjoy a licence to operate. Responsible business is, therefore, both an issue of individual firms' competitive advantage and about the enabling environment in which business collectively can operate.

Towards Environmental Sustainability
Jonathon Porritt

The author was the much-respected chief executive of Friends of the Earth UK before helping found Forum for the Future, the internationally recognised organisation promoting environmental sustainability and assisting major companies towards that goal.

One of the oft-quoted truisms of politics, journalism and management theory is that we live in an era of unprecedented change. Ask any business leader to list the greatest challenges facing his or her company in the next decade, and the reply is likely to include globalisation, e-commerce, European Monetary Union, and the instability of financial markets. For a few, somewhat further down the list, you would also find reference to today's environmental, social and ethical challenges – or sustainable development, to use the joined-up jargon!

What's more, the latter group are not just talking about sustainable development as an issue for the future, but in many cases are taking action right now. While it is true that one of the biggest problems we face in addressing this whole agenda is a powerful combination of complacency and denial (in both corporate and political circles), it is also true that some of the excessive negativity from environmental NGOs about the role of the business community can itself have damaging and disempowering consequences. Things have changed over the last decade, and are beginning to change even faster.

By any standards, there has been a remarkable evolution in the overall approach of the business community towards today's pressing environmental and social problems. From the publication of Rachel Carson's *Silent Spring* in 1962, through to the Earth Summit in 1992, the environmental battle zone rang with unending exchanges of accusation, insult and mutual misunderstanding. Confrontation was the name of the only game in town for the best part of 30 years, as the likes of Greenpeace, Friends of the Earth and WWF slugged it out with increasingly powerful multinationals. Governments somewhat inadequately sought to split the difference between them through accelerating programmes of new environmental legislation.

From the mid-1980s onwards, however, more and more companies were gradually coming to accept for themselves that the post-war period of 'economic growth at all costs' was coming to an end. The impact of what was in effect decades of 'licensed cost externalisation' had become much more visible; efficiency improvements in pioneering US companies such as 3M, S. C. Johnson and Proctor and Gamble were providing enough hard data to persuade business leaders that they too could start to clean up without any great commercial exposure. And the pace of regulation was hotting up all the time.

By 1992, building on the early work of the International Chambers of Commerce, the World Business Council for Sustainable Development (WBCSD) had convened an impressive array of business leaders to sign up to process of real engagement. They met in Rio de Janeiro, the week before the Earth Summit itself, focusing in on the business case for sustainable development, talking with increasing confidence and even enthusiasm for the notion of eco-efficiency:

> Eco-efficiency is the delivery of competitively priced goods and services that satisfy human needs and bring quality of life while progressively reducing ecological impacts and resource intensity throughout the life cycle to a level at least in line with the Earth's estimated carrying capacity.

There are, of course, all sorts of different ways of looking at eco-efficiency. Essentially, however, it is all about saving money by reducing material and energy intensity, by reducing toxic dispersion, by enhancing recyclability and extending durability, by maximising the use of renewables, and by increasing service intensity: the benefits a customer derives from the use of a product rather than the ownership of that product. Putting all these together, it is not at all difficult to get quite visionary about the possible consequences of a strategic engagement in this whole area of resource productivity.

Is the 2020 vision outlined in Box I.1 unrealistic? It depends how you look at it. Cliché though it may be, necessity really is the mother of invention. And necessity is what we are talking about here. We either learn to live

Box 1.1 2020 Vision

A spate of droughts, floods and other freak weather incidents in the closing years of the last decade has hardened the international consensus in favour of tighter limits on greenhouse-gas emissions. The groundbreaking Earth Summit 4, which took place in Birmingham in 2012, agreed a new 40 per cent global reduction target for 2030, against a 1990 baseline. The bulk of this will be achieved through absolute reductions, but the international emissions trading scheme, which was set up in 2003, will play a significant part. The success of the Clean Development Mechanism has enabled many developing countries to leapfrog straight to more advanced, non-polluting technologies.

Under the latest EU burden-sharing agreement, the UK's target has been set at 50 per cent. Fortunately, the UK's programme of ecological tax reform, which began at the turn of the century, has already stimulated a major shift towards clean technology and renewable energy ensuring that the new target will be met without any serious impacts on competitiveness. The UK's domestic-emissions trading scheme has been largely successful, and has helped to ease the transition to renewables for energy-intensive industries.

Tax incentives, which were put in place at the same time, have boosted the UK's share of the world-wide market for environmental technologies and services, which is now worth in excess of $1000 billion per year. These various measures combined are estimated to have created over 800 000 UK jobs in the past fifteen years.

The Labour-Green coalition government, which was elected in 2016, has continued the tradition of UK leadership on climate change and ecological tax reform, which began at the Kyoto Summit. Its most recent commitment is to match its 50 per cent carbon dioxide target with a 50 per cent renewable energy target for 2030. As the Prime Minister observed in this year's State of the Environment Address: 'Within ten years, the UK will be well on its way to becoming a solar economy'.

sustainably on planet earth (in which case, our survival prospects as a species are fine), or we do not – in which case, we become extinct. At that evolutionary level, there is literally no choice about learning to live within the earth's biophysical carrying capacity.

Such was the forward momentum of the Industrial Revolution, particularly in the phase following the Second World War, powered by access to cheap fossil fuels, that we pretty much ignored the physical limits to growth. Now we are beginning to feel the ecological pinch, with world population already at 6 billion and rising inexorably towards a 10 billion threshold by the middle of the next century.

It is that combination of surging population, the projected doubling of the global economy over the next 25 years or so, and a rapidly declining physical environment which makes all this so urgent. It goes without saying that business cannot possibly shoulder this responsibility on its own; it is governments that set the geopolitical and macro-economic frameworks within which companies create the wealth, and it is us (as consumers and citizens) who use our purchasing power and our votes for good or for ill. In essence, we need a new compact between business, government and civil society if we are to drive the transition to a sustainable future with sufficient purposefulness and urgency.

There are three broad categories of environmental policy which government has at its disposal: regulations, which lay down minimum standards of environmental performance; economic instruments, which give financial incentives to companies or consumers to reduce environmental damage; and voluntary agreements, whereby companies make commitments to improve their performance beyond the demands of the law. Good policy making will often use a mixture of instruments to address an environmental problem, but providing the right market signals is fundamental to influencing people's consumption decisions.

Arguably the greatest driver towards unsustainability is the way that conventional economics treats natural resources as inexhaustible and freely available goods. The costs of unsustainable activity are externalised, with the result that the price of goods and services does not reflect their true cost, and the market is distorted. Environmental taxes are the simplest way of balancing nature's books.

Research by Forum for the Future and Friends of the Earth in 1999 suggested that a gradual process of ecological tax reform would have a broadly positive effect on the UK economy. Based on sophisticated modelling techniques developed by Cambridge Econometrics, the research shows that if new or higher taxes on carbon, nuclear energy, landfill, incineration, aggregates, road fuel, company cars and car parking were gradually introduced by 2010, this could generate an additional £27 billion in annual tax revenues, create 391 000 additional jobs, and reduce carbon dioxide emissions by 12.8 million tonnes of carbon per year (a reduction of 7 per cent on the 1990 level).

Critics argue that environmental taxes pose a greater challenge to competitiveness than other policy instruments, but modelling the effects on a sector-by-sector basis reveals many more winners than losers. Provided the revenues from these taxes are recycled to business in some way, there is little evidence that the competitiveness of UK industry as a whole would suffer. Clearly, some sectors stand to gain more than others. Those which are relatively labour intensive will benefit at the expense of those which are more energy intensive. But provided new taxes are introduced at a pragmatic rate, allowing business time to change in line with investment cycles, this should not present a major problem.

If governments start to get the right mix of policy instruments, companies can then adapt their management, investment and product development strategies accordingly. And as our own experience in Forum for the Future has demonstrated so clearly (working with some of the real leaders in this area such as BP, Unilever, BAA, Interface, BT, Wessex Water and so on), it is that kind of transparent and long-term framework that makes all the difference.

The commitment to staff at all levels is vital if sustainability is to become part of the language and culture of an organisation. Strong signals from the boardroom are crucial in creating opportunities for action and innovation throughout the enterprise. This process has been termed 'vacuum management': just as a cyclist taking the lead in a race creates a vacuum into which other racers can slipstream forward, so a senior manager taking an organisation in a radical new direction creates a vacuum for others to fill with fresh ideas.

Education and staff training are particularly important if companies are to build ownership of the sustainability agenda at every level. Incentive schemes linked to improved environmental performance are a useful way of encouraging pivotal job holders to embrace sustainability. A handful of companies now include an environmental element in their systems of performance evaluation, and award bonuses if improvement targets are met.

As companies address the internal environmental challenge, so they must look outward to their stakeholders. The idea of 'the stakeholder company' isn't everybody's cup of tea; as Richard Koch puts it in *The Third Revolution*:

> the idea of managers balancing the rights of different groups of stakeholders and allocating resources to strike a fair balance between them – and this is the central idea of stakeholding, without which it is merely a set of exhortations for managers and corporations to behave responsibly – makes no sense at all unless there is to be a new decision-making apparatus which is different and better than the capitalist mechanism!

Even if it is only that – an exhortation to behave responsibly – a stakeholder approach of this kind at least takes some of the brutishness of conventional Anglo-American capitalism out of the mix, and enables companies to open up relationships of different kinds with many interest groups for whom that company might once have been a closed, no-go territory.

But none of this does terribly much to address an utterly unacceptable (and increasingly destabilising) level of global inequity. The 1998 UN *Human Development Report* revealed that 86 per cent of global expenditure on personal consumption is made by just 20 per cent of the world's people. The wealthiest fifth consume 58 per cent of total energy; have 74 per cent of all telephone lines; use 84 per cent of all paper; and own 87 per cent of all vehicles.

The implications of this are clear: over time, we must work to ensure that everyone has equal opportunity of access to the resources they need for a decent life. This idea has been powerfully articulated in the concept of per capita environmental space, which reflects the total amount of energy, non-renewable resources, land, water, wood and other resources that can be used globally or nationally without environmental damage, without impinging on the rights of future generations, and without restricting the rights of all people to a decent quality of life.

This challenge applies to business as much as to consumers themselves. As techniques of eco-innovation become more advanced, they will inevitably raise questions about the need for certain products, services or entire industries. Every company should be able to demonstrate that its products and services improve people's quality of life as well as generating a profitable return. Eco-innovation can go some way to reducing our unfair share, but it is vital that any 'extra' environmental space created is then used to improve the living standards of the world's poorest people. The social challenge of sustainability is to combine greater efficiency in our use of resources, with a new understanding of sufficiency in our attitude to consumption and quality of life.

Part I
The Route to Change

CHAPTER 1

From Earls Court to Victoria
Four Stations, 40 Years

It is a miracle we didn't meet at the beginning of the sixties. In 1960 we were both living in Earls Court, or Kangaroo Valley as it was then known because of the young Australians who, with a sprinkling of New Zealanders and South Africans, filled the majority of its bedsitters and pubs. John Egan shared a flat in Earls Court Square; Des Wilson lived in a tiny bed-sitter in the West Cromwell Road.

John, who was 20 in 1960, was studying at Imperial College (where he gained a degree in petroleum engineering in 1961); Des, who had left school in New Zealand at 15, was a cleaner at a jazz club by day and selling ice cream at Bertram Mills Circus by night.

We must have passed each other in the Earls Court Road scores of times, probably rubbed shoulders in the same cafes and pubs. In fact we were not destined to meet properly for another 35 years when John, now Chief Executive of BAA plc, recruited Des as Director of Corporate and Public Affairs. BAA's corporate office was, as now, at Victoria. We had, therefore, after all that time, only travelled four stations from Earls Court on the District Line. By then we were already each approaching the end of 40-year careers that could not have been in greater contrast and yet, for all that, ended on common ground.

John Egan, who was to become nationally known at Jaguar, was born into the motor car business: the family firm in Coventry was a Rootes dealership. John at 14 went to the local grammar school in Rawtenstall until the family moved to Coventry where he attended Bablake School. After his graduation from Imperial College he was hired by Shell International but after four years decided he wanted to learn more about business and went back to school, taking the first Master's business studies course at the London Business School, then part of the University of London, graduating with an MSc (the equivalent of today's MBA). He then joined General Motors where he had the opportunity to hone his management skills before joining British Leyland in 1971, where he eventually developed the company's spares and accessories operation, Unipart. In 1976 he moved on to Massey-Ferguson for whom he worked in Italy and Canada, and was well-established there when Sir Michael Edwardes persuaded him to return to British Leyland to take control of Jaguar.

According to John Underwood in his book *The Will to Win: John Egan and Jaguar*, when John arrived at Jaguar:

> the reputation of the company's cars was at an all-time low. They were seen, especially by the people who owned them, as poorly produced, poorly serviced, and likely to break down with frightening regularity.... It was said that Jaguar cars were the best thermometers in the world: the engine would start at 33 degrees F but never at 32 degrees ... that they were the perfect status symbol for the very rich because owning a Jaguar implied you could afford the heavy repair bills ... that the only way to keep a Jaguar on the road was to own two – since one would always be in the garage ... that Jaguar executives always lied about where they worked to avoid more jokes or abuse, or worse.

John is a firm believer in the power of brands. One reason he took the challenge was his belief that, for all its poor standing with Jaguar owners, the Jaguar brand still counted in the wider world. He insisted that Jaguar be freed from the shackles of BL and allowed to sink or swim as an independently run concern. The prospects were not encouraging; industrial relations (in the motor industry generally), workmanship and customer service were all appalling and the car was not selling. A meeting of distributors confirmed to him that the car was 'beautiful' but 'badly manufactured, badly assembled and badly serviced'. For what was not to be the last time John found himself urging his colleagues 'if we look after the customers, they'll look after us'.

Car owners were interviewed in their hundreds to identify the problems that needed to be tackled. Over 150 faults were found. John decided that the whole company needed to be re-orientated, with the priority being quality and reliability. Using the slogan 'in pursuit of perfection', he launched a company-wide campaign to promote quality. Task forces were set up to correct faults. Everyone, from board members to workers on the shop floor, was expected to get involved. It soon became clear that 60 per cent of the faults were caused by substandard components supplied from outside companies, so representatives of those companies were added to the task forces. Suppliers were pressured by financial penalties to improve quality or were replaced, but it was a 'carrot and stick' approach; suppliers were helped to improve quality and to see how to save money in the process. It worked; of the 1500 suppliers only a handful failed to achieve the required standards.

There are those who believe mission statements are just empty rhetoric. John believes they are the route map that enables everyone in a company to reach the same destination. As we will see later, at BAA the mission statement was distributed to every employee and debated at every management conference, and changes were made only when a majority of managers supported them. Whenever managers were debating what to do in a particular situation John would say 'well, let's go back to the mission statement and see what it tells us ... does this relate to the priorities or the stakeholders described there?' Although later at BAA he was to put safety and security top of the list, no Egan mission statement is complete without a pledge to satisfy customers and to enable employees to give of their best.

The phrase 'stakeholder companies' was not to become familiar for another 20 years or so, but it became clear to John even in those earlier Jaguar days that a number of groups had a stake, or, as he would have put it then, a vested interest, in the success of the company. There were the employees. There were the customers. But there were also the distributors and the dealers, and the suppliers. Only if they were all committed to what he wanted to achieve could he hope to win. This may seem so obvious now as to be not worth saying, but what he inherited at Jaguar was the opposite: disillusioned and unmotivated workers, indifferent suppliers, and distributors and dealers who had either become disenchanted with the unreliability of the car or worked in such a way that they impeded rather than contributed to success. John set about addressing each group in turn.

He invested a great deal of energy in uniting top and middle management with the work force behind a joint drive to re-establish quality. This involved an intensive communications and consultation exercise; for instance, groups of 300 workers were withdrawn from the production line to see a video on quality and then discuss the issues and make suggestions. Training programmes were upgraded. It was tough going at a time when relationships between the industry and its trade unions were at their worst, but John put his faith in a belief that, treated properly, the overwhelming majority of people want to take pride in their product and the company they work for. A quality product with a brand name to excite the market would be a unifying factor.

He also believes that the key to improving productivity is to encourage and enable people to bring their enthusiasm and intelligence to work. He encouraged the workforce to take part in various kinds of personal education programmes and 35 per cent did so. Many chose computer studies, while some buyers learned German to communicate with their German suppliers. The result of the internal and external education and motivational programmes was a 300 per cent increase in productivity.

Slowly but surely the faults were ironed out, suppliers and workers joined together in a drive to identify and eliminate every flaw, parts were made reliable, and Jaguar became once more a quality car worthy of its image. But now came the challenge of selling it.

Sales of Jaguar in the key market, the United States, had fallen steadily, eventually dropping from 8000 a year in the early 1970s to 3000 in 1980. Apart from its unreliability, which was now being overcome, the problem was the timing of production and delivery. Whereas in the UK the key date in car retailing is 1 August, when the annual new registration letter is introduced, in the US it is in September that the new, legally-updated models are introduced. Throughout the 1970s and 1980s Jaguar had consistently missed the dates; sometimes new models didn't arrive until April! Demanding that the customer become paramount, John set about identifying the causes and dealing with them. This included encouraging greater management discipline, but also investment in plant and machinery fit for the task.

The car now fit to sell and more likely to be available when it should be, John turned to marketing. John Underwood takes up the story in *The Will to Win*:

> Over several years the satisfaction that derived from owning a Jaguar car had been eroded. By 1980 there was no longer a pleasant sense of anticipation before a lengthy drive, rather the nagging fear of breakdown. A brilliant choice of colours was a thing of the long-forgotten past: if you wanted a Jaguar the choice was little more than white, yellow or red. Egan decided that the underlying mission that would inform all his actions at Jaguar was the restoration of customer satisfaction. It was the decision of a man who had set out

on a crusade to convert his company, its workforce and its management to being led by marketing rather than by production: 'If I had to single out one operating principle which permeates all our business activities at Jaguar,' Egan said, 'it would be satisfying customers.'

The first step in Egan's customer-orientation programme was to refine and develop the customer-contact scheme Jaguar had undertaken in 1980 to pinpoint the quality problems. Each month Jaguar would telephone 150 new customers to ask them what they thought of their new car, how they thought it could be improved and what they felt was unsatisfactory about it. They were also asked about dealer service and their impression of Jaguar as a company. The initial call was made just over a month after purchase; follow-up calls were made after nine months and eighteen months to see how the customer was getting on with the vehicle. The customer-tracking programme was so successful that Jaguar decided to start ringing the owners of rivals' cars: Mercedes-Benz and BMW drivers would receive telephone calls from Jaguar as the company tried to find out why they liked the wrong car, Egan said the research provided 'a wealth of priceless information'.

Jaguar also began carrying out regular public opinion surveys to determine whether people thought the company was well managed, profitable, old-fashioned, whether it marketed its cars professionally, had a sound future, cared about its customers, was conscious of quality and used modern manufacturing facilities. The importance of these surveys was that they helped the company understand its own public image, and that in turn helped it to understand why people bought Jaguar cars or indeed why they bought Mercedes-Benz, BMW, Porsche, Audi and Volvo.

It is never easy for any company to improve its relationship with its customers; it takes time and effort. For a motor manufacturer it is particularly difficult because apart from such selective sample surveys the company has no direct contact with its customers. Naturally enough, John Egan eventually turned his attention to the dealer network. As he saw it, the dealers were in the front line and they carried the responsibility for ensuring that Jaguar's good name was upheld: 'We certainly weren't going to let them treat that responsibility lightly.'...

He introduced strict minimum standards of service and customer attention that anyone holding a Jaguar dealership had to meet. He wanted exclusive Jaguar dealerships, he wanted smart, luxury showrooms; he insisted upon well-trained mechanics; he made sophisticated testing and diagnostic equipment a compulsory requirement; and if a dealer was not prepared to shape up and make the necessary investment he was replaced. The number of UK dealers was slashed by half. One hundred and fifty dealerships simply vanished and the remarkable thing was that Jaguar sales went up and up. It seemed that the customer was less concerned about the proximity of the nearest dealer and more concerned about the after-sales service he or she received....

A customer-contact programme was also introduced in the United States, carried out by the US automotive research company J. D. Power. Power's researchers actually recorded some of the conversations they had with Jaguar customers on audio cassettes and the catalogue of complaints made sobering listening. As they mused over the tapes, senior executives working for Jaguar's North American subsidiary became angrier and angrier. The recordings were distributed and used as a psychological tool to galvanize middle management. Many of the complaints proved to be about dealer service. When a dealer was found to have fallen down on the job he was told to make amends, but all too often no action was taken. Jaguar ended up accompanying customers to the premises of errant dealers and insisting that problems were put right on the spot.

Slowly but surely the message began to get through. Jaguar was no longer prepared to accept second-best from its dealers, from its suppliers, from its management, from its workforce. The customer-tracking programme gave the company chapter and verse on where it was going wrong but more importantly it demonstrated to everyone involved with the company that henceforth Jaguar was going to take the customer seriously. The people who were most impressed with the programme were the customers themselves, especially those who received the market-research calls. They began to feel they were important to Jaguar, valued clients whose views mattered. It must have been a truly novel feeling.

So far as Egan was concerned the customer was king. The customer-first gospel was spread in a host of different ways, with videos, posters, quality indices, quality circles and simply by word of mouth.

One of the most surprising things the company discovered was that improved quality did not necessarily lead to higher unit costs. Apart from the obvious warranty savings that resulted from fewer breakdowns, Jaguar executives also discovered that it was possible to build quality cars and components in a cost-effective way. It was largely a matter of planning and design. If a component was designed not just to fulfil a function but also for ease of manufacture, it often proved possible to offset the higher costs of quality with lower manufacturing costs....

Eighteen months later, when the earliest improvements had been made and when Jaguar was beginning to struggle out of the abyss, the company invited US dealers over to Coventry. Despite the groundwork the company had done on quality problems the dealers were still sceptical about just how much could be accomplished by Jaguar cars, but when they saw the transformation that had been achieved in attitudes and work practices, when they saw the pride and enthusiasm of the workforce they were genuinely astonished.... On their final night in Britain the US dealers were guests at a gala dinner. They were asked, during an after-dinner speech, if they could sell 9000 Jaguars the following year. (In 1981 the US dealers had taken just over 5000 cars.) They were so excited they bawled their agreement. Some were so enthusiastic they jumped up on their chairs and screamed, 'Nine thousand! Nine thousand!' Anticipating exactly that spirited response, Egan had arranged for the band of the Royal Marines to be waiting in the wings. As the excitement reached its peak the band marched into the dining room playing 'America the Beautiful'. The dealers scarcely believed such style and flair possible from their British cousins. They returned to the US fired with enthusiasm and began to sell and the following year saw them easily exceed the 9000 target. Michael Beasley believes that if the American dealers had not been won over, Jaguar 'probably would not have made it. So much relied on them taking those cars and having the confidence in us. In that respect it was a turning point.'

In the 24 months between the spring of 1980 and the spring of 1982 John Egan had got to grips with the main structural afflictions that had beset Jaguar Cars. Quality had been improved; supply timing had been given a degree of discipline; productivity had been pushed up ... and the crucial 'sharp end' of the cars business – the dealership network – had been made more profitable and more responsive to customer needs ... progress sufficient to see Jaguar transformed from a loss-maker into a company with a future.

John would like to be able to say that he took on the Jaguar challenge knowing already what the answers were. Much of what he did, however, emerged from the experience itself. By the time he left Jaguar, having led the flotation on the London Stock Exchange and then later the sale of the company to Ford, he had become – without fully appreciating it, at least in those terms – a committed stakeholder company man, firmly convinced that only when everyone who has a vested interest in the company's success is properly involved, their ideas incorporated, their efforts properly rewarded, can the company realise its full potential. He believed firmly that the employees had a stake. Their jobs depended upon the survival of the company; their rewards upon its success. It had to make sense to involve employees, to bring out their best, to unite them behind common goals. He believed customers had a stake; they were paying money for the product and they had to be able to rely upon it performing, and performing safely. They had worked for the money they were spending; they were entitled to value for it. Business partners – suppliers, dealers and the like – had a stake; a high-quality, saleable product was vital to their survival and success too. But not only did they have a stake in success, they also had it within their power to guarantee failure. Disillusioned and badly-motivated employees and suppliers had been producing for Jaguar a bad product; disenchanted dealers were not selling it; angry customers were giving it a bad name. Only by accepting their stake in success and their ability and responsibility to help achieve it did Jaguar recover.

If John left Jaguar with one stakeholder supreme in his mind, it was the customer. And it was this belief that he brought to BAA when he joined to become Chief Executive in 1991, and it was a creed that was to transform that company too.

BAA had formerly been the British Airport Authority; it had been privatised in 1986 but many of the old bureaucracies remained. Learning from the Jaguar experience, John went straight to the key external stakeholders: airlines and passengers. He found little in the way of customer orientation.

He used to get friendly letters from the chief executives of airlines asking for perfectly reasonable things. Then he would get a lengthy reply from a BAA manager explaining why the answer should be 'No'. He signed the first few and then, when another arrived, he telephoned the manager and said, 'Come on, they're asking for something very reasonable, why don't we just say "Yes"? Even a "Yes, but" is better than a "No".' He went so far as to say to one airline boss, 'Whatever the question, the answer is "Yes"'. Relations with the airlines improved dramatically and were reflected in a more positive response by them to BAA's regulatory review than would otherwise have been expected.

Basing his approach on the Jaguar lesson – 'If you don't know what else to do, start by satisfying your customers' – he now looked at the passengers' experience and concluded it was little short of appalling. These were the gateways to the UK and they were simply not good enough. Describing it later he said:

> We were stealing people's money. We supported a lot of little catering tricks. One was that you couldn't buy a cup of tea, you had to buy a pot. You couldn't buy a single whisky. The food was appalling and people were being robbed in the shops. You couldn't pay for parking less than two hours; that was a bad one. As for the car parks, they were like a journey into post-war Eastern Europe. I was going up the stairs one day when I asked the manager the cause of the smell and was told it was people peeing on the stairs. I said 'If they don't do it here, where do they go?' The manager pointed to a sign that appeared miles away. He said 'Over there, that's where they should go.' I said 'The customers have spoken, this is where they want to go. Put a toilet here.'

A campaign was mounted to improve customer service. Previously there had been a crude customer monitoring system covering about five issues, such as length of queues. It was replaced with an extensive quality-service monitoring system (QSM) involving interviews with hundreds of passengers every year on their experiences throughout their journey through the airport. QSM results were presented to the corporate management committee on a monthly basis and airport managing directors were expected to explain poor scores. The management bonus was directly affected by results. The result was a dramatic improvement.

Ironically one result of the poor customer service in catering and retailing was that the company was losing money in areas where it could make a profit. Once the catering and retail areas were brightened up and high-quality customer service and competitive prices introduced, they became highly popular and then highly profitable, eventually matching airport charges as a source of revenue for the company.

What John had found was millions of people having to spend time in airport lounges where they were trapped in an unwelcoming and soul-destroying limbo. By making them comfortable and giving them something to do, he not only raised their appreciation of the airports to the point where they began to win international awards but showed it was good for business.

To achieve all this of course he had to win the support of the employees. He introduced a mission statement and encouraged a nine-months consultation about it. Describing the overall challenge as to become the best airport company in the world, it set three key objectives:

- Always focus on our customers' needs and safety.
- Achieve continuous improvements in the profitability, costs and quality of all our processes and services.
- Enable all of us to give of our best.

Having also learned at Jaguar the importance of middle managers in either driving forward or thwarting any fresh initiative, John introduced a training programme called 'Sharing the Vision', and literally hundreds of managers experienced it. The aim was unity of purpose based upon shared learning of what lay behind the mission statement.

A two-yearly employee survey helped establish the workers' views on every aspect of the business.

After three years John had reason to believe that at least three of his stakeholder groups – employees, business customers and passengers – were reasonably on-side and that the benefit to that other key stakeholder, the shareholder, was clearly to be seen in consistently satisfying profits and dividends. Then, in 1994, an event occurred that was to cause John to recognise properly for the first time another stakeholder, and as a result lead to Des Wilson joining him at BAA.

We tell the full story of BAA's conversion to corporate citizenship later in this book; suffice to say that, despite major public inquiries and some local controversy, the company had never experienced too much difficulty in growing its airports. The public inquiries into a brand-new airport at Stansted and a fourth terminal at Heathrow had both been won, but it was already clear that getting permission to build a fifth Heathrow terminal was going to be more of a challenge. Some of the most vocal opponents were centred in Richmond and Twickenham: articulate, affluent areas affected by aircraft noise, where people were particularly upset by night flights.

John accepted an invitation to debate with Terminal Five (T5) opponents at a Sunday meeting in Richmond Theatre. When he arrived he was disconcerted to find himself faced with an audience of hundreds, and was even more disturbed by the strength of feeling. Being the subject of their anger for more than two hours was not a comfortable experience. Reporting this to colleagues the following day he said:

> Two things struck me. First, our opponents have up to now been portrayed to me as environmentalists or citizen activists. But these are ordinary people, our neighbours. They're not promoting an environmental or political cause; they're just upset by the noise and the traffic. We can't ignore this; these people have a right to be heard. Second, my guess is the rules have changed; we won't get permission to grow the airport by counting on a legal process, on technical arguments, or even on political influence; we have to carry the majority of the community as well and that means we have to listen to them and try and find an answer to their concerns.

John had discovered a new and increasingly powerful stakeholder: the airports' 'neighbours'. Now he had to discover a way to adapt the company so that it would acknowledge their existence and their concerns. As it happened he had planned to attend at that time a global travel and tourism conference in Budapest where the keynote speaker was Des Wilson, former chairman of Friends of the Earth UK and campaign director for FoE International, and now working in public affairs. Des was arguing the case for greater environmental sensitivity by the tourism industry, pointing out that:

> After all it is the environment you're selling; you who sell clean beaches and oceans, forests and lakes, places of natural beauty, surely have a vested interest in their conservation. You should not have to be pressured into environmental responsibility, you should be the leaders.

So, 35 years after our days in Earls Court, the authors of this book finally met. We spoke on the plane coming back to the UK and had lunch shortly afterwards. By coincidence BAA was looking for a Director of Corporate and Public Affairs. Des's career did not fit the profile but John by now believed that if the company was to overcome new challenges it needed a new-style public affairs advisor and communicator. He encouraged Des to make himself available.

Des Wilson was born into a working-class family in New Zealand, attended the local school, Waitaki Boys High School, and at 15 became a reporter on the local newspaper. After spells on the *Otago Daily Times* and the *Evening Star* in Dunedin, he joined a friend in Australia and worked on the *Melbourne Sun*. In 1960, while still only 19 and with only £5 in his pocket, he arrived in London and, after a few years surviving on all sorts of work and eventually returning to journalism, he was one of those who set up Shelter, the National Campaign for the Homeless, in December 1966. It became one of the country's best known charities, by 1970 having an income over £1 million a year, 350 local fundraising groups, and 40 housing groups helping homeless families in the inner cities. He then joined *The Observer* to write a campaigning column for over four years before taking time out to spend two years as Director of Public Affairs for the Royal Shakespeare Company (the theatre having been a passion of his since his teens).

In 1982 he returned to campaigning, this time in the environmental movement, combining leadership of the CLEAR campaign for lead-free petrol with the chairmanship of Friends of the Earth UK. It was with CLEAR that he found himself for the first time in confrontation with business and industry, and it was to have a profound influence on his views about business.

Contrary to the impression that may have been given by the ferocity of some of his and CLEAR's attacks on the lead-additive company Associated Octel and the petroleum industry at the time, Des has never been anti-business. On several occasions during the early 1980s he spoke to a number of industrial bodies, urging dialogue rather than confrontation. He frequently negotiated compromises with industries with whom the environmentalists were in conflict, arguing that the aim was not to weaken industry but to make it cleaner and more conscious of its environmental, health, safety and social responsibilities. In an article in the *New Statesman* he was later to argue strongly for greater understanding of the value of business and industry.

> At the latest count 20 560 000 people were employed in the private sector and 5 250 000 in the public sector. In other words four-fifths of those who work in the UK do so in business and industry, funding in the process the public and voluntary sectors where we find the remaining fifth ... so why is the word 'business' still virtually a swear word to many so-called opinion-formers? Why are so many public debates constructed around artificially-created confrontations between 'big business' and 'ordinary people' as if business is some amorphous entity, fundamentally hostile to human life, instead of a place where more than 20 million 'ordinary people' spend a fair chunk of their lives?

Despite all this, CLEAR's campaign was confrontational and for that Des blamed the extraordinary response of industry to the campaign's first approach. The background was that by the early 1980s all cars in the UK ran on leaded fuel and as a result considerable quantities of lead were being blasted into the atmosphere from car exhausts. A series of studies in the US, UK and Australia suggested that lead from petrol was the main source of lead-related environmental contamination, and that it was likely to have damaging effects – especially on children – at a much lower level than ever previously assumed. CLEAR was formed by a small group of scientists and concerned parents, many of them well known. The response of the relevant industries to their concern is described in Des Wilson's book *The Lead Scandal*:

> The petroleum industry in Britain has endeavoured since the launch of the CLEAR campaign to paint itself whiter than white. Its claims can be summed up as follows:
> 1. It is not qualified to comment on the health evidence, but will respond positively to whatever legislation is introduced. It is, therefore, neutral on the health issue.
> 2. It actually offered lead-free petrol to Whitehall in 1980–81 and was rejected, and cannot be blamed for the decision to reduce to only 0.15 grams per litre.
> In every respect, this position is duplicitous. During a court case,

the petroleum industry produced witnesses to directly challenge the
evidence of health risk. Furthermore, the petroleum industry owns
Associated Octel, who have been remorseless in their efforts to
claim there is no health risk whatsoever, and it has not attempted to
modify Octel's activities; on the contrary, Octel has steadily
increased its defensive activities and the petroleum industry has
been happy for Octel to do its dirty work.

On the question of whether it wants lead-free petrol, the petroleum industry has played a double game. It has never publicly
called for lead-free petrol, never assisted or supported the anti-lead
movement in any way, and in fact, has conducted a public relations
campaign calculated to present itself in the best possible light
whilst producing as many obstacles to lead-free petrol as it possibly
could. Unlike some petroleum companies in the United States, not
one petroleum company in Britain has produced lead-free petrol
before being forced to do so by legislation....

The whole history of this issue all over the world has been
marked by the fight of the petroleum companies against a ban on
lead. The US petroleum companies (many of them the same
companies operating in Britain) did all in their power to prevent
regulation or to have regulations overthrown. Clarence Ditlow,
chief of Ralph Nader's auto safety campaign in the United States,
says 'the oil companies fought lead regulation tooth and nail over
the years'. Their economic forecasts in several countries have
proved wildly exaggerated. The Australian Institute of Petroleum,
spent about $250 000 on a campaign to stop the decision to move
to unleaded petrol. A report by the Vehicle Emissions and Noise
Standards Committee said that early in 1980 the oil companies put
the transition cost at $400 million. This was later reduced to $300
million. Five months later it was reduced to $195 million. Still the
Committee found scope for significant reductions in the figure. It
concluded that the oil industry estimates were exaggerated more
than 10 times!

In West Germany, the petroleum industry estimated the cost of
reducing the lead levels in petrol to 0.15 grams per litre at DM 1000
million for modifications in refineries; all 25 refineries were
modified and the actual cost was well under DM 300 million – less
than a third of the figure the industry has projected. The German

petroleum industry warned of increased prices but the German delegation to the UN Environmental Programme seminar on the petroleum industry in 1977 stated that 'there was no basis to attributing any real price increases to the reduction of lead' and that 'as a whole it was found that the fears of negative consequences in various respects which had been canvassed before the decree was implemented proved to be greatly exaggerated'.

Prior to the final decision on the launching of CLEAR, on 9 November 1981, Des wrote letters to 10 leading British oil companies on behalf of 'a number of individuals concerned about the growing body of evidence of a serious health hazard arising from the use of lead in petrol', and sought further clarification of the individual companies' position and the answers to a number of technical questions. He also requested that the companies meet a deputation to discuss the issue further.

Not one of the 10 companies would answer the questions, or meet the deputation.

Every one of the 10 companies wrote an almost identical letter saying that CLEAR would be answered by the UK Petroleum Industry Association. (It took 10 weeks for the reply from the Association to arrive, and when it did, it consisted of a few trite phrases that could have been drafted overnight.) As Des wrote in *The Lead Scandal*:

What was astonishing was the communication that had quickly taken place between the companies, as reflected in the letters received.

For instance, Conoco Limited wrote: 'This is a matter that the UK Petroleum Industry Association keeps under review and I understand that they will be responding to you in due course.'

BP wrote: 'I understand you have addressed similar letters to other oil companies.... The Petroleum Industry Association will be replying very shortly with a full response to the points you raise.'

Shell wrote: 'The points you raise are being dealt with by the Petroleum Industry Association UKPIA; it is probably better that they respond and I understand that they intend to do so.'

A number of points need to be made about this.

First, while there probably is an overall industry point of view on this issue and there is no reason why the PIA should not state it, it is inconceivable that each company does not have its own view on any question affecting it, let alone a question of such importance. Furthermore no individual company can evade its own responsibility on issues of public health and safety.

Second, the similarity of the replies received from all 10 companies, together with open admission of knowledge by each company that it knew other companies had been approached and that the Association was responding on their behalf, shows the defensive mechanism which exists on the issue. It is disturbing that huge and wealthy companies, confronted with a simple set of questions from a private individual writing on behalf of other individuals, should mobilise such a well coordinated response. Their letters made clear that the telephones buzzed between them and their Association. If they do this in reply to one letter, from one person, it is worth asking what defence mechanism they set up when they feel themselves under real pressure – for instance when they are faced with enquiries from Whitehall?

Third, the refusal of all 10 companies to even consider meeting a deputation on a matter of such deep public concern reflects their priorities and the little time they are prepared to set aside to communicate with people other than those who – we must assume – can contribute to their profits.

Fourth, the only possible assumption that can be made is that all of the companies were concerned that they should not inadvertently make a concession on the economics and technical details that would contradict the centrally-organised line of the public-relations-orientated UK Petroleum Industry Association.

At the same time as Des wrote to the petroleum industry in 1981, he also wrote with a list of questions to car manufacturers. The first point to be made about the replies generally was that the car manufacturers did at least respond more openly than the petroleum industry. British Leyland, however, took the same position as the oil industry, namely that the public health question was not for the industry to consider. One firm, Talbot, attempted the same approach as the oil companies: 'I feel your questionnaire can be better handled on an industry-wide basis. Accordingly perhaps I could suggest you contact the Society of Motor Manufacturers and Traders.' Reliant wrote that 'a letter without formal heading from a private individual, rather than an association … does not necessarily warrant a great deal of time or attention'.

Des was later to sum up the approach of industry to the CLEAR campaign at a number of major conferences, notably one in Toronto organised by the Mars company:

> First, not wanting to hear the message, they attacked the messengers, describing the campaigners as hysterical, emotive, anti-industry. Of course the environmental movement has its extremists, but there are extremists in every form of human organisation, including business. Organisations deserve more than to be judged by their extremes. The fact is CLEAR was motivated only by knowledge of the science on this issue and concern for children. In an American journal a director of Associated Octel was quoted as saying about CLEAR: 'It's probably supported by anti-capitalists. We can only see three reasons for the anti-lead movement: support by precious metal producers who want catalytic converters (the lead makes these ineffectual); support by engineering groups who believe they will have new facilities to install; or support by leftist-sponsored, anti big business groups. We think the third is most likely.'
>
> In other words, we were either being paid to get lead out of petrol to help another industry … or we were anti-industry. Genuine motives were apparently out of the question.
>
> It never crossed the petroleum, car-manufacturing, or lead additive industries' minds that the families that lived near roads and were exposed to lead pollution had a 'stake' in their businesses. Yet they did. They had a stake because the product of those businesses was a threat to the health of their children. They had a stake in a technically-possible and affordable alternative, lead-free petrol, that would relieve them of their concern and of the danger. Nor did it cross the industries' minds that these stakeholders were a powerful force, often well-educated and articulate voters who, when it came to their children's health, were ready to be mobilized.

The result was a vocal and persistent campaign that finally even Margaret Thatcher could no longer ignore. So the campaign was won within 15 months and ultimately succeeded in a decision to remove leaded petrol from the whole of Europe. Des was later to conduct a campaign in his home country of New Zealand; it was won in nine days! For him the lasting memory was the behaviour of the industries involved: their refusal to accept any responsibility for the polluting or public-health effects of their actions; their contempt for – and attempts to discredit – the environmentalists or concerned parents; their attempts to buy their way to success with lobbyists and influence in the corridors of power.

Des still argues that he was never anti-car or even anti-industry in this campaign, merely concerned to right a wrong. As soon as the decision was taken, CLEAR joined in a working group with civil servants and industry to establish the most cost-effective way of moving to lead-free petrol. On this group former opponents became colleagues.

A further lesson in the importance of addressing the stakeholders' concerns was to be taught to the UK retail trade when, after his time in the environmental movement and two years planning and then running the Liberal Democrats' 1992 General Election campaign, Des took on the role of campaign advisor to the major retailers seeking to change the trading laws so that people could shop on Sundays.

Armed with a supportive Royal Commission and backed by a majority of over 100 in the House of Commons, Margaret Thatcher had sought to introduce Sunday shopping in 1986, but a combination of small shop-keepers, trade unionists and Sunday observance campaigners had defeated even her. Now the retailers were making another attempt, but this time John Major was in Number Ten with a majority of less than 20. Des remembers attending a meeting in the office of David Sainsbury, then chief executive of the family firm. Also there were the heads of Asda, Boots, Tesco, Kingfisher, Dixons and a number of other High Street giants. He was astonished to discover they were still hoping to achieve total deregulation of the Sunday trading laws. 'How can you hope to do it with a weak PM and a small majority when you failed with a strong one, backed up by a Royal Commission and a huge parliamentary majority?' he asked.

When asked to suggest a solution he listed the key stakeholders: small shop-keepers who relied on their trade early on Sunday mornings; shop-workers who were afraid they would be fired if they did not want to work on Sundays for family or religious reasons; and church leaders who had enough trouble attracting a congregation without competing with the supermarkets. Each of these stakeholders could mobilise support in the House of Commons. Des argued that only by listening to them and addressing their concerns could the case be won.

In addition to that meeting Des toured the boards of these companies, speaking to their directors. After much debate and with considerable reluctance, the retailers decided on two compromises. First, they would seek only partial deregulation, namely opening hours from 10 to 4, thus reserving the precious earlier hours for the smaller shops and also protecting the early morning and early evening church service times. This satisfied most Conservative back-benchers. Second, they would sign a workers' charter, guaranteeing security of employment to those who for any reason didn't want to work on Sunday. That satisfied the trade unions and Labour back-benchers.

The result of this campaign, built upon a coalition established by the Shopping Hours Reform Council, was a historic vote to allow Sunday trading in Britain, carried through in much more difficult political circumstances than in 1986, but achieved because the companies had listened to the stakeholders and addressed their concerns.

So it was that when we two, businessman and former campaigner, met over lunch after our meeting in Budapest, the conversation quickly turned to the lessons in all this for BAA and whether it was possible to initiate a campaign to change the company in order to acknowledge the new community stakeholder. The company was by no means a dinosaur when it came to its stakeholders. John's emphasis on satisfying customers, developing better partnerships with related businesses, and engaging the minds of all employees had already achieved considerable success. And at least some of its managers, and its public affairs professionals, understood that it had to change its approach to the community as a whole. But in this area it was still in its infancy. BAA was not yet a corporate citizen. That had to change. How we set about it, the mistakes we made as well as the successes we achieved, form a major part of this book.

For us both there was much at stake personally. John had the responsibility of leading BAA into the twenty-first century and to growth. He knew that only by changing the company could he succeed. Des knew that unless the company changed radically he would have joined a company that was part of the problem, rather than part of the solution; his own self-respect as an environmentalist (let alone his reputation) would be in ruins. But this was a chance to show there was common ground and that real results could be achieved if an environmentalist worked from within.

This was to lead to an exciting and encouraging five-year partnership, with each other, and with colleagues who also enthusiastically embraced the concept. We do not claim a miracle. We accept that by the end of the five years we worked together the company had made only a start. It takes time to change the culture of a company, carrying with you not only the employees and shareholders but also business partners, and it is not always easy to change complex practices and work processes. But it is immensely satisfying to see a company that previously was unknown in the world of corporate citizenship now emerging as a leader and winning international awards. Mike Hodgkinson's current drive to persuade the whole industry to adopt sustainability now takes the company's activities onto a higher plane of ambition. Nor do we claim that what was achieved was the result only of our own efforts. Far from it. Many others within the company, not least Richard Everitt, its director of strategy and compliance, Chris Hoare, its first Community Relations Director, Andrew Currie, his successor, and Kathryn Barker, its environmental manager, worked tirelessly to drive the concept forward. They were encouraged by a new generation of airport managers including Janis Kong at Gatwick, and by the airport public affairs teams.

This book does not, therefore, purport to be the case history of a success, but rather an account of our experiences and the lessons we have learned. We hope it will prove helpful to others setting out on the same path.

In researching it, and in communicating with and sharing experiences with other companies and with the organisations promoting corporate citizenship, we have also become aware of just how much change is taking place. Of course it is controversies (whether about real or perceived scandals) that hit the headlines, and we record some of them in the next chapter, but what we found was a growing movement within international business and industry towards a new kind of inclusive, socially-responsible stakeholder company. So profound is the change that is occurring and so critical is it to the achievement of harmony between business and the community, to the benefit of both, that we have termed it 'the twenty-first century business revolution'– a revolution we entreat our readers to join.

CHAPTER 2

The Twenty-First Century Business Revolution
The Rise of the Stakeholder Company

In June 2001 the *Observer* newspaper published a leading article urging its readers not to buy petrol at Esso garages. Under the headline 'Join the boycott against Exxon now', it accused the company of being a key player in persuading the Bush administration in the United States to abandon limits on carbon dioxide emissions and thus to reject the Kyoto accords on global warming.

> It is time for Britain to drop our softly-softly approach to corporate social responsibility. The public wants better. We should have a legal framework in which companies report openly on their ethical, environmental and workplace policies so that consumers can chose those with which they wish to be associated. This is already being done by some firms, notably BP and Shell. The *Observer* does not believe either is perfect but neither behaves like Exxon and both support the principle of the Kyoto accords. If *Observer* readers want to take direct action over climate change they should buy their petrol from these companies and not from Esso. Don't put a tiger in your tank.

This unusual recommendation from a serious newspaper demonstrated both the business benefits of being seen to do the right thing and the danger facing companies that do not. BP and Shell stood the chance of winning extra custom – in other words, a business gain; Exxon, one of the world's biggest companies, was threatened with the loss of a billion pounds a year in the UK alone – a business loss. And that's not to talk about the damage to its reputation; one in ten MPs signed an early day motion supporting the *Observer*'s call, and such well-known personalities as Bianca Jagger, former Conservative Secretary of State John Gummer and Anita Roddick backed Greenpeace and Friends of the Earth campaigns. The company launched a public relations counter-offensive but it was ineffectual; fair or not, Esso was now being associated with corporate irresponsibility, while BP and Shell emerged with improved public standing.

If the board of Exxon was surprised by all this, it should not have been. After all the same company had suffered an earlier catastrophe in terms of public opinion, also at the hands of environmentalists, when its oil tanker the *Exxon Valdez* spilled 11 million gallons of crude into the fragile Alaskan ecology of Prince William Sound in 1989. The public outrage in the US was unprecedented. Scenes of environmental devastation flashed into living rooms across the nation – crude oil washing onto 1300 miles of coastline with a huge marine death toll. The company ended up spending over $2 billion cleaning up, as well as at least another billion to meet claims, and lost millions more as consumers went to rival companies to fuel their cars. This was clear warning that the environmental movement could not be easily brushed aside; Exxon's clash with it over the Kyoto accords showed it had not heeded that warning.

But if Exxon should not have been surprised by the latest campaign, Shell and BP had reason to be both surprised and gratified. Six years earlier Shell had been devastated by the Brent Spar affair, perhaps the most famous ever enforced about-turn by a major international company in the face of environmental protest and consumer boycotts. (We will return to that episode later.) Then Shell's operations in the Niger Delta led to an embarrassing crisis for the company. When the Ogoni people, native to the region, protested against pollution from leaking pipes and demanded local control over oil revenues, the leader of the protest, writer Ken Saro-Wiwa, and eight others were tried on what appeared to be trumped-up charges, found guilty and hanged. While Shell argued it had played an economically helpful role in the country and did plead for clemency for the activists, a spokesman inadvertently fuelled the criticism by appearing to limit the company's sense of responsibility to the country it was working in:

> We believe our role as a responsible Nigerian company is to work with the communities in our areas of operation to complement and add value to this central core of government-driven development.... We believe our most effective contribution to Nigeria is through the taxes and royalties we pay and the wealth we generate for the economy.

This at least appeared to make social and environmental responsibility a secondary concern, if that. Furthermore, said critics, there was little evidence that the wealth generated reached much beyond the politicians and civil servants themselves. Writing in the *Daily Telegraph*, the highly-respected environmentalist Jonathon Porritt, a constructive bridge-builder with industry, reflected the outrage felt by many observers:

> With the execution of Ken Saro-Wiwa, it is hard to ignore the stain of blood now spreading down that once-proud [Shell] corporate logo. To wash its hands of the events which left him dangling at the end of General Abacha's noose, as Shell now does, is morally despicable.... The torture and killings go on. Yet Shell's main priority has been to sign an agreement with General Abacha for a brand-new £2.5 billion natural gas plant.... It is a long time since I felt compelled to weigh in like this. But part of my anger is that Shell is exactly the kind of company that bridge-building environmentalists like me are now keen to work with.

Protests, including a major one led by pension-fund-holders at the Shell AGM, finally led to the company promising a fresh approach to environmental and human rights issues. It now has an impressive code of conduct and social responsibility programme.

BP, too, had not been without its critics, despite the progressive leadership of John Browne, one of the more outspoken supporters of greater corporate social responsibility at the top of a company in the FTSE 100. Only weeks before the 2001 anti-Esso campaign began, the BP annual general meeting had been confronted by human rights campaigners. Supporters of the Free Tibet campaign, they attempted to force the company to break off links with a Chinese business partner alleged to have supported China's occupation of Tibet. Also at that AGM were environmentalists who had become shareholders specifically in order to protest at the company's plans to drill in the Arctic. BP also became the subject of a critical article in the *Independent on Sunday* for allegedly contributing to the election funds of congressmen 'with the worst environmental records'. Whether the charges and complaints were fair or not, the company had found itself back in the dock at the court of public opinion.

Yet now, at least temporarily, these two companies, Shell and BP, were receiving popular support, if only as an alternative to Esso.

By the end of the first year of the twenty-first century no-one in the oil industry, whether under attack, as was Esso, or at least temporarily approved of, as in the case of BP and Shell, should have been in any doubt; there were external influences over their affairs they could no longer ignore: organisations and people who as campaigners could damage their reputations and as consumers could refuse to buy their products. And they would never go away. Managing a business had changed forever.

The year 2001 had already been a noteworthy one for those who believed that those major companies and industries that had not done so should review their relationship with the world around them. For instance, the huge and powerful pharmaceutical industry had been forced to make a humiliating withdrawal from an action in the South African courts to protect their patents, a defeat at the hands of anti-AIDS campaigners that, as the *Guardian* suggested, 'they may come to regret, not only because of the damage to the industry's reputation but also because it may result in the severe weakening of the patent rights they are trying to protect'. This was a significant confrontation and even some critics of the pharmaceutical industry doubted whether it would prove a socially helpful outcome in the long term, especially if it discouraged spending on research. What it showed, however, is that even the firepower of this industry could not overcome outraged and provoked public opinion.

A variety of other major companies and whole industries on both sides of the Atlantic had on either side of the turn of the millennium found themselves under public pressure over some perceived or real sin. Some began to learn the lessons. Notable was a comment by a Microsoft lawyer who was involved in the major confrontation between that company and the US courts over alleged abuse of monopoly: 'We have already learned a lot – about our responsibility as a corporate citizen, about our responsibility as a business partner', he admitted. European industrialists got together and planned a campaign for corporate social responsibility, aiming at a 'CSR year' in 2005. Major companies like Proctor and Gamble, General Motors and Shell signed up to a Global Reporting Initiative (GRI), a voluntary programme encouraging integration of economic, environmental and social performance reporting. UK environmental minister Michael Meacher led a governmental drive to encourage companies to sign up to GRI; at an awards event in London, he promised to 'name and shame' companies that would not respond, but he also recognised the growing number producing high-quality corporate responsibility and sustainability reports. The regulators in the UK were also beginning to take a grip; the Turnbull Committee on corporate governance demanded that companies report on how they were going to handle social, environmental and ethical risks; changes to the Pensions Act in 2000 made it compulsory for trustees of pension funds to report on these three areas of risk in their annual publications. The European Commission published recommendations that companies should recognise, measure and report on environmental issues in their annual reports. Finally, in 2001, the UK Company Law Review encouraged stakeholder accountability. Those initials 'CSR' (corporate social responsibility) began to appear everywhere on business pages of the national newspapers and in business and industry publications. Corporate social responsibility, corporate citizenship, stakeholderism and sustainability found themselves on business conference agendas, then the subject of seminars in their own right. It is fair to say that by the end of the first year of the twenty-first century these concepts were rapidly becoming accepted by any company that aspired to be described as progressive. Wrote John Elkington, leading commentator and advocate of corporate citizenship, in September 2001:

> In a dramatic trend affecting most rich world economies, new forms of corporate accountability are emerging…. Some companies may still chose to go against the flow, but the trend is clear: a process of corporate and wider economic transformation has begun.

The trend has, of course, been there for some time, but its rise has been slow. Until recently many boards still saw this as a trend that, like many before it, would come and go, perceiving corporate citizenship as an expensive luxury or an indulgence. They only accepted its relevance when their own actions were challenged and, even then, they often sought a public relations solution, a 'cosmetic' response, rather than addressing genuine concerns and trying to find true answers to real issues. Some are still lagging behind. Perhaps this is because there are still many directors in that generation whose gurus were of the old school. 'Business ethics is an oxymoron, a contradiction in terms, like jumbo shrimp', commented a leading business publication as recently as the mid-1980s. And for some highly respected gurus the idea that companies should be motivated by any factor other that profit was not only laughable; it was subversive. Thus Nobel Prize winning economist Milton Friedman:

> When I hear businessmen speak eloquently about the social responsibility of business in a free enterprise system … that business is not

concerned merely with profit ... that business has a social conscience, and takes seriously its responsibilities for providing
employment, eliminating discrimination, avoiding pollution, and
whatever else may be the catch words of the contemporary crop of
reformers, [I say] they are unwitting puppets of the intellectual
forces that have been undermining the basis of free society.

Safety

For decades, as the first citizen groups began to emerge and try to enforce
higher ethical standards on companies, boards would argue that the law and
the regulator were the definers of what they should and should not do. All the
rest was 'politics – and business is not about politics, it is about profit'. This
notion that the law was the limit of a company's ethical responsibility was first
significantly challenged by the case of the Ford Pinto, marketed in the late
1970s. The model had been involved in a succession of fatal accidents in
which the petrol tank exploded after the car was struck from behind. In 1978,
following a crash in which three young women burned to death, the company
became the first in corporate history to be indicted for reckless homicide. In
court, the company's lawyers argued that because the model met all applicable
safety laws and regulations, the company had met its obligations to society,
and it was cleared of criminal charges. But in the court of public opinion, the
outcome was different. As a contemporary commentator pointed out, there
were widespread misgivings that the company had not acted ethically:

> that there had been some weighing of a known risk alongside the cost
> of eliminating it.... Students who study the Ford Pinto case today
> understand that business ethics is not the same as complying with the
> law. The law provides the floor, or the lowest agreed upon standard
> below which no one should go. While laws are intended to be ethical
> and to be based on some consensus of what is right, ethics is a much
> broader category. Ethics is the study of what is good and right for
> people. Ethics is about not causing unjustifiable harm. It is about
> only doing what you would be willing to be done to you.

The motor industry had in fact first been confronted by consumer pressure
back in the 1960s. When Ralph Nader emerged on the scene in the US to
challenge General Motors, the company was humbled by exposure of its

efforts to discredit him. Nader led a new and highly effective consumer movement for greater emphasis on health and safety. If Nader's campaigns on car safety touched the first nerve, in the US in the 1960s, later in the UK it was two disasters on Britain's privatised railways that strengthened the public's perception that private companies were capable of putting profits before public safety. In 1997 seven passengers died when a Great Western Intercity passenger train went through a red signal and collided with a freight service on the approaches to London's Paddington Station. The passenger train carried an automatic warning system which would have prevented the disaster, but after developing a fault it had been turned off. The train had run without the system, even though the equipment in a rear locomotive was operational. Using it would have meant turning the train around and delaying the service. In October 1999, the public was stunned when an almost identical disaster happened just outside Paddington. This time, 31 people died and 400 were injured when a Thames commuter train collided with Great Western Intercity service after going through a red signal. The Thames train had not been fitted with the advanced ATP safety system, allegedly for cost reasons. Lord Cullen's report described a 'lamentable failure' to heed warnings about risks of accidents in the area.

Rewards

Apart from corporate performance on safety, the last decade of the twentieth century witnessed a growing interest in what was and was not fair in terms of reward for work, and this was reflected in widespread criticism of alleged corporate greed.

'Greed is good. Greed is right. Greed works. Greed clarifies. Cuts through and captures the essence of the evolutionary spirit.' If anything captured the ruthless excess of the late 1980s it was this speech by Gordon Gekko, the character played by Michael Douglas in Oliver Stone's *Wall Street* (1987). The film struck a chord with a public who believed that Gekko characters had come to life in the boardrooms of the country's privatised public utilities. Labelled the 'fat cats', they appeared to be lining their pockets at the expense of the people who had trusted them to run public services like gas, electricity and water for the good of the nation.

The UK's most notorious symbol of perceived corporate greed was Cedric Brown, Chief Executive of British Gas, a company which was the second most admired in 1984. Its slide from grace began in the November of that

year, when it revealed that Brown was getting a pay rise of 75 per cent from
£270 000 to £475 000. In fact even after the salary increase he was well down
in the surveys of top executive pay, and many believe was particularly badly
advised, but coming days after the company announced an increase in
charges for some of its customers, the news produced a fire storm of critical
media coverage. That was just the beginning; in what appeared to be an
exercise in crass insensitivity, British Gas alienated one stakeholder after
another: gas showroom employees on £13 000 per year were told they would
have to take pay and holiday cuts; shareholders, already angered by the
Brown affair, learned that further pay rises were on the way for top managers;
and there were reports that British Gas was cutting the money it spent on
checking for gas leaks.

The anger grew when senior executives of the national electricity distribution company, National Grid, were alleged to have avoided tax by
transferring shares to their wives. This was a perfectly legal measure, but
the media was in a critical mood. The *Independent* noted that:

> Like true Eighties men, they could not understand what all the fuss
> was about, as they went about the business of making as much
> money as fast as they could. The free market was operating, so all
> was well as far as they were concerned…. Meanwhile, the rest of us
> looked on angrily, fed up with a bunch of characters who did not
> seem to know the difference between right and wrong. The issue was
> not whether the tax wheeze was legal. What mattered was that it
> failed to pass the Nineties test. It was not fair. So the executives
> should not have behaved in the way they did…. The row demon-
> strated the great cultural gulf that has opened up between most
> people and those who run industry…. Suddenly, those who sit in …
> boardrooms are looking like yesterday's men and women. They do
> not understand how much Britain has changed. People now want
> more than the simplistic liberal economics that those who forged the
> Eighties revolution proclaim. They are not hostile to capitalism, but
> demand that business should also operate according to certain addi-
> tional ethical standards. They want integrity and high-mindedness.
> Companies must not only be profitable. They should also be good.

The utilities were to be ruthlessly punished for all this. The Labour Party,
taking advantage of their unpopularity, announced it would hit them with a

windfall tax if it was elected. When it was, in 1997, it did just that, taking billions of pounds from the privatised companies, whether they were guilty of bad behaviour, as was British Gas, or well-behaved, as we believe BAA was. Gordon Brown could never have imposed this retrospective tax if the utilities had not so wrong-footed themselves with the public.

In the US, CEOs who had presided over brutal downsizing in the early 1990s faced similar criticism when they were seen to be reaping rich rewards. *Business Week* reported in 1996 that:

> Many believe that the new generation of lean, mean, cost-cutting executives possesses no sense of shared sacrifice – once thought to be a sacrosanct ingredient of leadership. Indeed, the CEOs of the nation's most downsized corporations last year displayed a near in-your-face defiance of the notion that they should make even the smallest symbolic offering to share the pain. The CEOs of the 20 companies with the largest announced layoffs last year saw their salaries and bonuses jump by 25 per cent, well above the average. Add the value of new stock-option packages granted to these same CEOs in 1995, and the increases are often staggering.

The gap between CEO and average pay was widening: 'In 1980, the boss's average paycheque was a mere $ 624 996 – 42 times the pay of the ordinary factory worker. By last year, the multiple had grown to 141.'

On both sides of the Atlantic, whether or not companies could justify the pay of their CEOs by their performance or the threat of losing them to rivals, uncomfortable juxtapositions were being made with the plight of the companies' other stakeholders. Barclays Bank fell into this trap in March 2000 when it announced 6000 job losses and the closure of over 170 branches at the same time as a substantial rise in top executive salaries and bonuses. The media and shareholders were severe in their response. By 2001 every pay increase, bonus or issue of share options to a chairman, chief executive or senior board member, was being noted by the media and commented upon by the City and by shareholders. At more and more AGMs chairmen were being faced with awkward and embarrassing questions, above all about pay-offs to chairmen or chief executives who were said to have failed. The Secretary of State for Trade and Industry Patricia Hewitt was forced to warn that tough measures would be taken if there was no restraint.

Here the employee as stakeholder, and the shareholder as stakeholder, were having their say. But so was society as a whole, itself a stakeholder in the sense that the issue touched on the concept of social justice. When considering what they paid themselves, boards were having to consider carefully 'how it will appear outside'. In doing so they were acknowledging that their reputations, their standing with the public as a whole, were relevant to their business well-being. In this area too they were becoming accountable to public opinion.

Exploitation of the Vulnerable

Another major issue, especially for multinational or global business, was the alleged exploitation of Third World countries by companies who found that, by going to poorer regions desperate for help, they could pay low wages and evade tough health and safety regulations and other constraints in their own countries. The American chemicals company Union Carbide forced the issue to the top of the corporate agenda in 1984 when a deadly cloud of toxic gas escaped from its plant in Bhopal, India. 2500 members of the local community died and 200 000 suffered injury and ill health in what remains one of the worst industrial accidents in history. 'The Bhopal plant did not meet American standards, according to Union Carbide's own inspector, and had not been inspected by headquarters auditors in two and a half years,' reported the *New York Times*.

A number of major world-wide brands became the target of charges and critcisms for their alleged behaviour in the Third World. For instance, the food giant Nestlé faced similar criticism over the marketing of its breast-milk formula to an unsophisticated market in developing countries. Poor mothers, critics argued, would be better off breast-feeding, particularly in areas where the water which they needed to mix with the product was likely to be contaminated. Without proper sanitation, babies were said to face three times the risk of dying from a respiratory infection, and 25 times the risk of dying from diarrhoea. Nestlé was accused of increasing the risks to babies by encouraging mothers to use its baby-milk substitutes and for much of two decades the company became the target of an international consumer boycott because of the issue. The boycott was suspended in 1984, when the company agreed to implement the World Health Organisation international code of practice, requiring all marketing of breast-milk substitutes to promote the benefits and superiority of breast milk and the health hazards of using substitutes unnecessarily or improperly. But in 1989, after

accusations that Nestlé was contravening the code, the boycott was rein-
stated. The campaign continued, and in 1999, Nestlé faced the ignominy of
a ruling by the UK Advertising Standards Authority that a statement in one
of its advertisements could not be supported. The statement was simply
this: 'even before the WHO International Code of Marketing Breast-milk
Substitutes was introduced in 1981, Nestlé marketed infant formula ethically and responsibly, and has done so ever since'. *Marketing Week* reported
the ruling as 'a first class public relations disaster ... which effectively
brands the global corporation a liar insofar as it claimed to have marketed
infant formula products ethically'.

During the mid to late 1990s, other well-known companies found themselves targets of embarrassing allegations that their suppliers in developing
countries employed workers in sweatshop conditions. But it was a sweatshop
scandal on American soil that swept the issue to national prominence. In
August 1995, Federal and state officials raiding an apartment complex in El
Monte, Los Angeles, discovered 72 Thai women working against their will
behind razor wire. The apparent return of slavery to the US stirred public
outrage. The media spotlight turned to pay and working conditions in Third
World sweatshops contracted to top multinational companies. The name that
came to symbolise the scandal was Nike. For an international brand investing
millions in its public image, the front page of a *New York Times* in November
1997 must have made grim reading:

> Undermining Nike's boast that it maintains model working condi-
> tions at its factories throughout the world, a prominent accounting
> firm has found many unsafe conditions at one of the shoe manufac-
> turer's plants in Vietnam. In an inspection report that was prepared in
> January for the company's internal use only, Ernst and Young wrote
> that workers at the factory near Ho Chi Minh City were exposed to
> carcinogens that exceeded local legal standards by 177 times in parts
> of the plant and that 77 percent of the workers suffered from respira-
> tory problems. The report also said that employees at the site, which
> is owned by a Korean subcontractor, were forced to work 65 hours a
> week, far more than Vietnamese law allows for $ 10 a week.

The tone of media coverage on the sweatshop issue became increasingly
hostile towards Nike, and a boycott of Nike products affected sales during
the Asian crisis – a time when the company could least afford it. Nike

introduced codes of conduct and a radically-changed regime and, addressing the US National Press Club in 1998, company CEO Phil Knight acknowledged the public mood:

> It has been said that … the Nike product has become synonymous with slave wages, forced overtime and arbitrary abuse…. I truly believe that the American consumer does not want to buy products made in abusive conditions.

Recently Naomi Klein's powerful book, *No Logo*, attacking the behaviour of multinational companies in the Third World has become a best-seller. She may be excessively cynical about the positive steps companies are taking to address international concerns over human rights and other issues, and she under-plays the essential role business has to play in helping to solve many of the most acute Third World problems, but just the same her book has represented a case to answer.

Environmental Issues

The main focus for the growing confrontation between 'big business' and the citizen has been concern for industry's impact on and use of natural resources. Clearly the greatest global concerns are global warming, increasing desertification with consequent loss of water and land to grow crops, and the loss of forests and species of animal and plant life. All of this is both made worse by, and itself makes worse, the problem of Third World poverty, famine and disease.

The environmental movement is, of course, not new, but its political impact has only really been felt over the past 20 years. In the early 1980s the CLEAR campaign for lead-free petrol represented one of the first major victories for the environmental movement across the whole of Europe. The Green Party became a major force in Germany, and by 1989 the Greens were attracting 16 per cent of the UK vote in the European elections, humiliating the Liberal Democrats who won only six per cent. The environment movement was moving from the fringe to the centre of political (with a small 'p') life. In the US hundreds of thousands turned out for the 1990 Earth Day. 'The United States may have come late to the green movement … but nobody could fault it now for lack of zeal', reported the London *Times*. Industrialised countries began adopting tougher legislative and regulatory control of corporate behaviour. In 1992, the Earth Summit in Rio de Janeiro brought the principles of sustainable development into the lexicon of popular environmentalism, and it was this agenda that companies increasingly found themselves having to address.

In the UK, the £ 2 billion a year national road-building programme – a key commitment of the Conservative government's election manifesto in 1992 – encountered growing resistance as ancient woodland and wild-flower meadows were seen to be sacrificed to 'the great car economy'. Once more this was not as straightforward as it appeared; for instance, those who opposed a by-pass could in fact be condemning a town to excessive pollution or heavy traffic that was damaging to both its physical and social fabric. At the same time, demographics – producing a more elderly population – as well as the inadequacies of public transport to meet the needs of rural dwellers meant there were often powerful social reasons for road-building. But, of course, there are good and bad ways doing things, and road-building plans appeared at times insensitive to genuine environmental concerns. Tiny pockets of countryside became household names. 'For the last week it has been a war zone', reported the *Guardian* from Twyford Down in Hampshire, site of the M3 extension.

> Keats's beloved chalk down, an Area of Outstanding Natural Beauty which English Heritage have called 'the most important archaeological landscape in southern England', is as theoretically protected as any place in Britain with two Sites of Special Scientific Interest, ancient monuments, burial mounds and Celtic field systems betraying evidence of people living there for more than 3000 years. Yet at one end there now lives a conscript army of 100 private security men, paid for by contractors Tarmac Construction and the Ministry of Transport.

At Twyford Down and the battlegrounds that followed it, a new generation of 'eco-warriors' chained themselves to bulldozers, took to the trees and burrowed into tunnels, joined in some cases by quite 'respectable' Middle Englanders. (Incidentally, the Twyford Down controversy was not necessary; tunnelling under the Downs, while more expensive in the short term, was clearly viable as an ecologically satisfactory solution.) The protests came to a head at Newbury in February 1996, when thousands of protesters walked along the planned route of the town's controversial by-pass and achieved massive TV coverage (local people, who by a clear majority supported the by-pass, did not achieve the same level of publicity).

If the roads protesters were new to controversy, so were their targets – private companies like Tarmac at Twyford Down and Costain at Newbury, whose contracts, as far as anti-road protesters were concerned, had turned them into instruments of environmental destruction. The message had already struck home at Tarmac. After its bruising experience of direct action by protesters at Twyford Down and on the floor of its AGM, the company announced the creation of an environmental panel of independent experts to monitor its activities, and effectively ruled itself out of the running for the Newbury contract on environmental grounds: 'As a responsible company, we have told the government that we can no longer go on like this,' said John Banham, non-executive chairman of Tarmac. The company, he explained, would only take on the Newbury contract if the government used inde-pendent environmentalists to advise on how to mitigate its worst effects. (The company later became an environmental award winner.) When Costain won the Newbury contract, it found itself the target of concerted activism: Friends of the Earth administered the purchase of shares to give its members a voice at shareholder meetings, while protesters published lists of Costain premises to be targeted on 'anti-Costain days'. The company's chief executive found banners in his garden at home.

Newbury was further evidence of a palpable change in the public mood that had begun the previous year with another environmental issue: Brent Spar. This is now so well documented an episode that it has almost become a cliché in the debate, but such was its impact that we cannot ignore it. When Shell announced it was going to dump this huge floating buoy in the deep ocean, Greenpeace launched a major international campaign to stop them. Although Shell had the full backing of the British government, and of tech-nical and scientific opinion, and in our view was probably doing the right thing, it never stood a chance once Greenpeace mobilised public opinion. A consumer boycott of Shell service stations temporarily cost the company market share, particularly in Germany where the public was most hostile. To the fury and embarrassment of the British government, Shell buckled under the pressure. The Brent Spar did a U-turn in mid-ocean that came to symbolise a turning point in the attitude of companies towards their stake-holders. In a series of full-page advertisements in the German national newspapers, the recalcitrant German subsidiary of Shell tried to patch over its damaged reputation: 'We are going to change', it told its customers. 'We have learned that for certain decisions, your agreement is just as important as the opinion of experts or the approval of the authorities.' The *Independent* commented:

> For those who are concerned about environmental degradation, the Shell case will provide a great fillip. It is now clear that neither governments nor big business are strong enough to withstand a new phenomenon: an alliance of direct action with public opinion. Greenpeace deserves the credit for mobilising a political force that we can now expect to grow in power and have an impact on a host of other environmental issues. Their volunteers informed the public and highlighted the problem. But the crucial element that changed Shell's mind was not the actions of those who landed on the Brent Spar platform and obstructed the dumping. The deciding factor was the ability and willingness of ordinary people to boycott Shell products.

These words echoed through the years and other environmental conflicts, but at the end of the decade they found particular resonance with one company: Monsanto. Its engineered seeds offered farmers increased crop yields and lower pesticide costs, and in the US they embraced the technology. By 1998, 38 per cent of the soya beans and a quarter of the corn planted was GM. Anxious environmentalists tried to stop the GM juggernaut in the US, but they were largely ignored. If the American Food and Drug Administration said GM foods were as safe as their non-bioengineered counterparts, that was good enough for the average American consumer. In Europe, it was a different story; health scares such as BSE in the UK had dealt a heavy blow to public confidence in scientists and the authorities. When environmentalists appeared to be getting a sympathetic hearing in the British media, Monsanto launched an aggressive advertising campaign to promote the benefits of GM technology. Instead of easing concerns, it provoked a backlash in which the company and its CEO, Bob Shapiro, became the symbol of an industry that was increasingly represented as a threat to public health. In 1998, two internal Monsanto reports, leaked to Greenpeace, described how public opposition to GM technology was 'sky-rocketing'. 'At each point we keep thinking that we have reached the low point … but we apparently have not', wrote the author, Stan Greenberg. In 1999, the crisis deepened as the collapse of European consumer confidence in GM foods lost Monsanto's farming customers valuable outlets for their crops. In the UK, the *Daily Mail* catalogued a stampede away from GM:

> The rush to avoid so-called 'Frankenstein food' has intensified in recent weeks, despite Government reassurances that GM food and crops are safe. All the major supermarkets have recently promised to go GM-free including Sainsbury's, Tesco, Safeway, Asda and Marks & Spencer – following pressure from customers. Their lead has been followed by fast-food firms and more recently food manufacturers, including Unilever, which owns Van den Bergh and Birds Eye Walls.

Monsanto survived its association with Agent Orange and chemical warfare in Vietnam', commented the *Independent* in April 1999. 'But when Robert Shapiro chose to apply the science of genetics to improving crops, his company became demonised as the dark force behind "Frankenstein Foods".' The attacks left their mark on the Monsanto CEO. In October 1999, he was described as looking 'pale and drawn' when he addressed a Greenpeace conference. What he said revealed a company chastened by its public mauling: 'Because we thought it was our job to persuade, too often we've forgotten to listen. Our confidence in this technology and our enthusiasm for it has, I think, been widely seen, and understandably so, as condescension or indeed arrogance.'

Note that his concession was about the way the company had handled the issue, not about GM foods as such, for even some of those who have changed their behaviour in response to public protest will argue to this day they were merely bowing to public perceptions and prejudices rather than reasoned or scientifically-proved argument, and undoubtedly a feature of many of the cases described above is that even now it cannot be assumed the protests were justified. There are still many who believe the Shell plan for Brent Spar was the right one. There are many, including British Prime Minister Tony Blair, who remain unconvinced about concerns over GM foods. There are those who would argue the Newbury by-pass has done far more good than harm. We will return to this issue later; suffice to say for the moment that we record these episodes as influential ones. If they did not convince the companies and industries concerned that they were acting wrongly, it must surely have convinced them – as it clearly did Robert Shapiro – that they were account-able to public opinion and needed to enter into proper discussion and debate in the new context of a greatly changed citizenry who, if they were not properly informed or consulted, or felt they were being treated with arrogance, would use the blunt instrument of public protest, consumer boycotts, reputation-damaging propaganda and so on to force the companies into the open. That increasingly well-educated and self-confident citizenry were forcing a change in the rules within which business and industry operated. And it was right that they did so. Responsible companies had little to fear from this; the irresponsible had lessons to learn, not least the willingness of ordinary people to exercise their stakeholder power. Whether customers, investors, voters, local residents or employees, these stakeholders are able to strike businesses where it hurts, and advocacy groups have become increasingly adept at mobilising their power.

The Customer

In today's marketplace, consumer decisions are increasingly influenced by the values associated with the brands and companies behind the products. The more at odds these values appear to be with those of their customers, the more likely they are to walk away. In a MORI opinion poll, 17 per cent of people in the UK said that they had boycotted a product on ethical grounds in the previous twelve months. But keeping in tune with the values of customers is just part of the market sensitivity expected of today's companies. Customers are more demanding in every sense: in addition to expecting companies to behave well in an environmental or human rights sense, so they expect them to behave properly as providers of goods and services. They expect more information about products, higher standards of quality and safety, better value for money and the right to return their purchases if they have changed their minds; they are prepared to take ruthless advantage of wider choice, and are unforgiving when companies get things wrong. Today the consumer, with more choice than ever before, is truly king.

Towards the end of the 1990s this became increasingly apparent in the cases of two of the UK's top blue chip companies: Sainsbury's and Marks & Spencer. Complacent in their success, they began to take their stakeholders for granted; M&S, finding growth difficult in the UK, became over-absorbed with an attempt to develop internationally; Sainsbury's allowed themselves to be drawn into a market-share battle with their up-and-coming Tesco rival, and put at risk in the process their reputation for high quality and wholesome products and services. Both, their critics claim, had at least temporarily simply lost touch with their main stakeholders, their customers, and their profits and share prices plummeted.

Carphone Warehouse boss Charles Dunstone has been one of the new breed of retailers taking on the older-established companies with a passionate commitment to customer service: 'If you don't look after your customers and employees, then ultimately you'll run out of people who don't know how bad you are,' he told *Marketing* magazine.

Employees

As Dunstone implies, employees are another stakeholder group now increasingly influencing the behaviour of companies. Employees in the UK may these days be far less likely to exercise their right to take industrial action, but the impact of labour disputes on individual companies can still be devastating. The particularly acrimonious dispute with its cabin crew faced by British Airways at the end of the 1990s did much to damage the company's blue chip image and contributed to a slide in its popularity and profitability. With high levels of employment in many industries, today's employees are far more likely to use the sanction of leaving companies they don't respect. They increasingly expect to know what their employers know, to participate in decision making, to be empowered to achieve the best for themselves and their company, and to share in the rewards. Companies that fail in these areas are finding themselves losing out in the competitive marketplace for good staff. After de-layering and downsizing, employees are less loyal and more mobile than ever, and in the growth sectors of the economy they are also more difficult to attract and retain.

Although remuneration is still an important factor, employees are increasingly motivated by non-financial issues. For example, in two surveys conducted by Gemini Consulting and Coopers and Lybrand, the need to balance work and personal life was identified as the top employee issue. Opportunities for training and lifetime learning are also high priorities. Stakeholder companies in tune with the concerns of their staff clearly have an advantage over their competitors. A company's public reputation also has a significant bearing on its attractiveness to potential recruits. People want to be able to identify with their employer, to feel proud when they tell their friends who they work for. It is well catalogued that the brand-conscious graduate market is particularly sensitive in this respect.

Shareholders

Shareholders, too, are exerting more power. Today they expect more information, more often, more quickly. And like customers, they hold the sanction of 'walking away' if they are not happy. Under company law, they also hold the ultimate sanction over directors, though, as we have seen, the big fund holders who hold the real power rarely use it. The swelling ranks of shareholder activists are also making their mark on corporations. AGMs have become platforms for shareholder advocacy; from the irreverent or disaffected small shareholder, to corporate governance watchdogs like the Pensions Investments Research Consultancy (PIRC), which advises its pension fund clients on formal resolutions. Shareholder advocacy has also become a staple of pressure groups like Friends of the Earth and Greenpeace, who use the shareholdings of their members or sympathetic groups to table resolutions in the same way. The Company Law Review, published in 2001, if reflected in enforced or voluntary change, will radically alter the balance of power between company and shareholder in favour of the latter.

We referred to BP earlier: in April 2000, a group of 100 British and American BP-Amoco shareholders with 150 000 shares tabled a formal motion at the company's AGM opposing its Arctic Ocean exploration plans and the construction of the Northstar oil pipeline, and proposing that the company should redirect the capital to solar manufacturing. The 100 shareholders were gathered together by Greenpeace, the US socially responsible investor Trillium Management Corporation and US Public Interest Group (PIRG). They may have been outvoted but they were forcing the board to defend its actions publicly and giving notice that such issues would always now be on the company's agenda.

The expansion in the number and range of ethical funds has been driven by public activism, as investors seek to avoid companies they do not like, and to back companies they do. In the UK, demand for ethical investments is also being driven by pension schemes whose trustees are required to disclose 'the extent to which social, environmental or ethical considerations are taken into account in the selection, retention and realisation of investments'. Institutional investors are being advised by PIRC through its Corporate Responsibility Service, which looks for opportunities for wealth creation in companies with 'high standards of excellence' in their relations with key stakeholders. In May 2000 the *Financial Times* reported that

Friends Provident was to put its £15 billion worth of assets in equity port-folios behind 'the global campaign to force companies to embrace good practice in human rights, child labour and environmental pollution'. Its chief executive was quoted as saying 'Good corporate practice (in these areas) is good for society but it's also good for shareholders'.

The Dow Jones Sustainability Group Index has consistently outper-formed the broader Dow Jones Global Index by 15 per cent since the beginning of 1994. 'Sustainability provides a unique investment style', explains David Moran, President of Dow Jones Indexes. 'The performance of companies implementing sustainability principles is superior because sustainability is a catalyst for enlightened and disciplined management, a crucial success factor.' An example of this enlightened approach is the streamlining of business processes to reduce energy and water use and to eliminate waste. The result is a contribution to conservation of resources and reduced corporate costs: the classic 'win–win'. Another example is the way progressive companies manage their supply chains. Turning their backs on the old adversarial system, they have developed long-term constructive relationships with their suppliers, secured by a commitment to give them a certain level of business. This sense of shared destiny in the supply chain fosters teamwork. Suppliers lend their expertise to other parts of the process, and with a guaranteed level of business they have the confi-dence to invest in new plant and equipment; they are also prepared to be more flexible, allowing clients to carry less inventory; the result is a better product, streamlined processes and lower costs.

The Twenty-First Century Business Revolution

These are just a few of the groups of stakeholders and issues that compa-nies have been learning to respond to. Hardly a day goes by when another controversy is not reported in the newspapers; 'case law' grows. A library of books detailing these cases is rapidly developing; hence our decision to review them only briefly. Our desire is to move on to more positive ground. For, slowly, as controversy has followed controversy, and one major company after another has become publicly entangled in disputes over the effects of its behaviour either in its own country or internationally – over its impacts on health and safety, human rights and the environment – many have developed a belief that they have to approach their business from a wider perspective, accepting responsibilities for much more than the 'bottom line'. They accept, in essence, that they should think and act like full and caring citizens of the community.

In the nineteenth century we had the industrial revolution. In the twentieth century we had at least two huge human resources changes: first, greater industrial equality driven by the rise of the trade unions and Labour movement, then in turn greater employee involvement as management came to understand that it needed to harness the employees' brains as well as their brawn in order to remain successful. Towards the end of the twentieth century we also experienced the information and technological revolution, whose full outcome is probably still beyond our imagination to appreciate. Now, at the beginning of the twenty-first century, we have a revolution in the way business perceives itself: no longer a law unto itself, but now accountable to the community and its highest values. In the world of business and industry it is a revolution in thought and deed. In terms of the ongoing freedom for industry to realise its full potential for creating wealth and improving the quality of life for people everywhere, this revolution is as crucial as the earlier ones.

One of the concepts to emerge (and in the UK to be taken up by the Blair Administration in the late 1990s) was stakeholderism. The word recalled the days of the American settlers who drove a piece of wood – a stake – into the ground to claim their territory. In the same way, said the theorists, companies were associations of claims and counter-claims by 'stakeholders' with a vested interest in a business: employees, customers and investors among others, who had a right to be considered. It was the job of the companies' managers to arbitrate between their competing claims. This definition was gradually widened to what one commentator described as 'any group or individual who can affect, or is affected by, the achievement of a corporation's purpose'.

It is extraordinary how many highly intelligent businessmen could not see the logic of the stakeholder approach. After all, by the last 30 or so years of the twentieth century most understood that if you treated employees well, motivated them with proper incentives, involved them, gave them a 'stake' in the company, you would get better performance and this would be reflected in better quality work and greater productivity. All but the incurably stupid understood that if you cared about your customers and sought to satisfy them, they would return and buy more, and this was good for business. Some understood that the better you treated your suppliers, the better they would perform for you. And, of course, they all understood that if they did not keep the shareholders happy, they would not be able to finance their businesses. So most sensible business people already understood that there were at least four groups with a serious interest in the company – its employees, customers, business partners and shareholders – and that it served the company best to live in harmony with them and their concerns. Why, then, was it so difficult to extend that understanding to other, social, stakeholders, notably neighbours, the local community and the countries the company operated in?

Perhaps it came down to the fact that employees, customers, suppliers and shareholders could all directly enhance profit; it called for more effort to understand that so could these wider social stakeholders. Perhaps it was a reflection of traditional business education, both academic and through work experience. Perhaps it was that the appearance and language of the environmentalists and other citizen activists encouraged an assumption that they represented a political assault, a challenge to private enterprise or capitalism itself, so that it was possible for business people to draw a line between those who were basically 'on side' and those who were 'anti-business'. (If so, then the environmental and citizen action movements must bear some responsibility for this, as Jonathon Porritt suggests.)

The fact is that the world was changing and many people engaged in business were so focused on their own company and industry that they could not see it happening. In particular the middle class had become more powerful: better educated, more confident and more articulate. A high proportion also had high ideals; this was the generation that fought for civil rights in the 1960s, that founded the environment movement, that protested against the 'military/industrial complex'. They may now have mortgages to pay and kids and wealth to protect; but the middle classes have been far more willing to challenge authority than their conservative predecessors. In most cases this challenge was not 'political' in the traditional sense but a reflection of educated values, of access to information about environmental and other effects of products and types of corporate behaviour. The vast majority wanted a high standard of living, would vote for economic growth, but wanted the products they bought to be clean and safe, and the companies that supplied them to be socially and environmentally responsible.

This, as we will discover in the next chapter, is what John Egan and BAA found with respect to the growth of Heathrow. A huge majority of local people told opinion pollsters that they valued the airport, they understood its importance to the economy, and they wanted to be able to fly. But as local residents they also wanted to feel safe, to sleep at nights, and to have their concerns about traffic and air pollution listened and responded to. They were calling for balance.

People had a new confidence to fight for themselves; the days when they automatically assumed that 'I can't change this' had ended with the rise of a better educated and more articulate citizenry strengthened by the forces of technological change. For the average person in the early 1990s, the main source of information about companies was the media; now they have the Internet and a world of information at their fingertips, from the companies themselves, from the electronic media and from advocacy groups. Advocacy group websites are bringing people with similar values and interests together in virtual communities. Able to communicate with members directly, advocacy groups are finding it easier to mobilise and coordinate support for shareholder activism, consumer boycotts, direct action and other kinds of protest. The fact that mainstream media are also connected to these sources of information increases the potential for local issues to escalate into national and international stories within hours. Whether they are consumers, investors, members of local communities or employees, today's stakeholders are getting more information about companies, more quickly. The more global a company's operations and markets, the more sensitive it must be to local issues and how they will be perceived elsewhere. It is arguable that if Shell had been more sensitive to sentiment in the German market, it would not have treated the Brent Spar as a 'British issue' and not found itself so isolated; if a manufacturer such as Nike had adopted each country it worked in as its own, extended its sense of corporate pride to its behaviour everywhere, not just where it was noticeable, it would have avoided the sweatshop scandal; and if Monsanto had not made its decisions only in the US but been more understanding of consumer sensitivities in Europe, it would have handled the GM issue differently.

One of the reasons the Western world at the end of the twentieth century had largely abandoned war as a way of achieving national objectives, largely rejected racial prejudice and refused to tolerate blatant environmental pollution is because the basic values and concerns of the overwhelming majority of peaceable and fair-minded people have been so effectively articulated and mobilised within democratic systems as to make the behaviour of the past more difficult. Now, at the beginning of the twenty-first century, many young people around the world are being mobilised again, this time on the issue of globalisation of business. Riots at international conferences in Seattle,

Gothenberg and Genoa were forcing international leaders to question whether it was worth holding these events at all. As we have noted, the emergence of this new 'cause' and new breed of protester is chronicled in the best seller *No Logo*. You do not have to share the author's negative verdict on international business, nor wish to encourage the kind of protests she clearly feels to be legitimate, to accept that she represents a widely held view that calls for a decisive answer. That answer has to be a practical and relevant response to the human and social problems that underpin the charges being made. Fortunately that response does exist – in the twenty-first century business revolution.

Definitions

As enlightened companies and progressive consumer campaigners and environmentalists began to unite around the need for dialogue and a way forward that all could live with, four concepts have emerged: corporate citizenship, corporate social responsibility, sustainable development and stakeholderism. We are often asked what are the differences, and of course there are strands that run through the centre of all four. These include: accountability to the wider society; respect for, and attention to, the concerns of all those affected by or with an interest in the company and/or industry; and a sense of environmental responsibility.

- **Corporate citizenship** we would define as a recognition by the company that, like every individual or group in the community, it is 'a citizen', both benefiting from the strengths that come with community and accepting the duties or obligations that go with membership of it. An illustration: a company that refuses to accept its citizenship obligations may decide, without care or consultation, to expand its business with no concern for any damage to the community or environment; a corporate citizen company will inform and consult and negotiate its growth, and will seek to make positive contributions that balance any negative impacts it may have to ask its neighbours to accept.
- **Corporate social responsibility** we would define as accepting that a company's concerns should go beyond the bottom line to the health and well-being of the world it belongs to, seeking to reflect society's highest values, protect its environmental bounty, show respect for human rights and be a positive contributor in the widest sense to the community. This

responsibility extends beyond the local community to the country as a whole and the world beyond. An illustration: a company with a genuine sense of social responsibility would not observe the highest safety standards at home while exploiting the economic vulnerability of the Third World by abandoning those standards in its plants there. It would make every plant a matter of corporate pride, a symbol of hope, not a thing to be endured for minimal local economic gain.

- **Sustainable development** is about finding ways to develop a business or industry without permanently damaging the environment or depleting the world of non-renewable natural resources; as a UN report once put it, 'meeting the needs of the present without comprising the ability of future generations to meet their own needs'. It carries social responsibility beyond the short-term interests of today. An illustration: a logging company will probably be acting sustainably if it balances its tree-felling with a progressive forestry programme involving extensive re-planting. If it chops a tree down, it should plant another.

- **Stakeholderism** is about identifying every individual or group that has either a specific direct interest or an indirect interest in the activities of a company and communicating, cooperating and combining with them to the benefit of company and stakeholder alike. Direct stakeholders are the company's owners, its shareholders, its employees, its customers and its business partners. Indirect stakeholders include neighbours and local communities, but may also comprise whole countries and societies. An illustration: as we shall see in the next chapter, the airport company BAA is regulated and has to be responsive to its aviation industry stakeholders; it has passenger customers, employees and shareholders, and has to be accountable to them all; it also has to pay regard to local communities and national and local governments who have planning and other powers. These all have a stake in the company's behaviour and performance. They are entitled to influence, to expect their concerns to be addressed. But their support can also provide the company a licence to do what it wants and/or needs to do.

As we have argued, there are strands that run through all of these concepts and we would be happy to be described as advocates of any of them. We have chosen to put our emphasis on stakeholder companies in this book because we believe this concept, with its assumption that all who are affected by the company, directly or indirectly, will be accounted to, as the best way to focus a company on exactly what it needs to do. Corporate social responsibility and corporate citizenship are good and worthy concepts; stakeholderism is in our view the most practical expression of both of those aspirations.

Rise of the Stakeholder Company

In the UK in 1993, a lecture at the Royal Society of Arts (RSA) by Professor Charles Handy entitled 'What is a Company For?' inspired an RSA inquiry into the qualities that would make a company successful in the future. After consulting more than 8000 business leaders and opinion formers, it published its findings in 1995. To be successful, the report said, tomorrow's company would have to be able to answer four questions about itself: Why does it exist? What does it have to do to succeed? Which relationships are crucial? What needs to be measured in order to sustain success? Profit and the creation of long-term value for investors remained crucial, but tomorrow's economy needed to find new ways to generate these returns. Understanding stakeholder needs and incorporating them into business strategies was central to this quest. This 'inclusive approach' emphasised building long-term positive relationships with customers, suppliers, employees, shareholders and the community. Traditional adversarial relationships would have no place.

It would be foolish to deny that the twenty-first century business revolution has initially been inspired by the kind of controversies and harsh experiences referred to above (and, of course, we could have quoted many other cases), or that many companies have been forced to change while others have noted the headlines and heeded the warning. That does not matter. What matters is that the revolution is happening, still fairly slowly, but with momentum, and that it is bringing together traditional business people and the most progressive and sensible campaigners. In the UK in 1996 the Centre for Tomorrow's Company was created to take the inclusive agenda forward within UK business, joining other organisations such as Business in the Community, Forum for the Future and uniting some of the most brilliant of their generation of environmentalists – Jonathon Porritt, economist Paul Ekins and former Green party activist Sara Parkin – in a drive to bring out the best in business. John Elkington's SustainAbility also became increasingly influential. Similar organisations have sprung up in Europe and the US. These organisations provided (and still provide) a supportive infrastructure to business as it entered the twenty-first century revolution. Case studies began to emerge of companies, small and large, that were finding a stakeholder approach to be immensely beneficial to their business, but also to the world around them. There are now inspiring stories of banks investing in the kind of poverty-ridden ghettos that financiers previously ignored, to the benefit of both bank and local community; of companies that boost profitability by making genuine stakeholders of their employees; of businesses that achieve a dramatic increase in market share by the way they newly embrace their customer stakeholders; of companies that find new ways of doing things to avoid pollution and environmental damage; and, above all, of FTSE 100 and Fortune 500 companies revolutionising their relationships with communities and countries, sharing their concerns, accepting their values, and making themselves properly accountable. Some still falter from time to time, some still have a lot to learn, and others are yet to make a beginning. But the revolution is under way and there can be no going back.

Speaking about Shell's experience with Brent Spar, Eric Faulds, the then decommissioning manager responsible for the platform, identified the need for stakeholder dialogue:

> Many people simply did not know about the complex issues involved, and we had done little in advance to explain them.... We accepted that we needed to engage on such issues in a much wider political and public domain. We also accepted that there could be real limitations to the 'decide, announce, defend' approach in which decisions are taken by 'authorities' or 'experts', announced to interested parties, then followed by what may be confrontational debate between proposers and objectors.

In 1996, Shell asked its stakeholders what they thought of it in the light of the Brent Spar affair and the execution of Ken Saro-Wiwa. The consultation involved 7500 members of the general public in 10 countries. Half the responses were either neutral or unfavourable and 10 per cent of people regarded the company as uncaring about the environment and human rights. 'We ... looked in the mirror and neither recognised nor liked some of what we saw', the company admitted. In 1997, the company published a ground-breaking report, 'Profits and Principles – Does There Have to Be a Choice?' in which it spoke frankly about what it had learned from its stakeholders:

Multinationals have been criticised as being overly concerned with profit and failing to take their broader responsibilities seriously: to defend human rights, to protect the environment, to be good corporate citizens. Such accusations reflect a shift in what society expects of both business and government.... This debate is taking place in the context of a fast-changing world, characterised by global communications and diminishing respect for established authority, professions and social frameworks – a form of moral vacuum in which fear and doubt prosper. Faced with such uncertainty people are withdrawing their trust in traditional institutions unless it can be demonstrated that such faith is warranted – what has been called a move from a 'trust me' to a 'show me' world.

Another multinational facing up to society's changing expectations was the mining company Rio Tinto, for many years the target of protests by indigenous peoples. In the old days, admitted the company's Chairman, Robert Wilson, there was:

a systematic weakness in those areas where things went wrong for us ... a tendency to be over reliant on the law as a means of resolving dispute. This sort of approach ... really does not work in communities which may neither accept nor understand the law of their governments. And even if they do accept it, they certainly won't respect it if it fails to recognise their own traditional way of doing things.

Rio Tinto redefined the way it should interact with its local communities based on the principles of mutual trust, active partnership and long-term commitment. Noke Kiroyan, President Director of Rio Tinto Indonesia, explained the business logic behind the building of long term relationships:

While community development is a noble undertaking in itself, we cannot ignore its more practical aspects.... In establishing peace with the community, mining companies are then free to go about their business without fearing interference in the form of social disturbances, which inevitably lead to decline in productivity and result in losses.

John Browne of BP described how the company reconciled its business with sustainable development.

> BP accepts that it has a responsibility to act. We're therefore taking specific steps: to monitor and control our own emissions; to support existing scientific work and to encourage new research; to develop experiments in joint implementation and technology transfer; to develop alternative fuels for the long term; and to contribute to the public policy debate in search of the wider global answers to the problem.... To be sustainable, companies need a sustainable world. That means a world where the environmental equilibrium is maintained and where the whole population can all enjoy the heat, light and mobility which we take for granted and which the oil industry helps to provide. I don't believe those are incompatible goals. All the actions we're taking and will take are directed to ensuring that they are not incompatible.

In response to the sweatshop scandal, Nike launched six initiatives to improve factory working conditions. These included increasing the minimum age of footwear-factory workers to 18 and the minimum age for all other light manufacturing workers (apparel, accessories, equipment) to 16, and strengthening environmental, health and safety standards, including the adoption of US Occupational Safety and Health Administration indoor air-quality standards at all footwear factories.

Companies are accepting the need to demonstrate their commitment by reporting their progress openly and submitting to external monitoring and independent validation. Standards such as Social Accountability 8000 (SA8000) and AccountAbility 1000 (AA1000) have emerged to offer additional confidence that a company's ethical declarations are more than PR puffery. The Global Reporting Initiative (GRI) is providing the basis for comparing the performance of companies.

Corporate giving clearly cannot 'buy-off' obligations to behave ethically in the course of everyday business, but it remains fundamental to today's stakeholder company. Between 1994 and 1999, charitable donations from the UK's FTSE 100 companies rose 54 per cent to an average of 0.22 per cent of pre-tax profits. Though this is well below the US average of 1 per cent, the growth is likely to accelerate with the introduction of new tax breaks. The nature of corporate giving is also changing. From old-style arm's-length philanthropy, it is moving on to a more strategic footing, as companies increasingly regard donations as a social or community investment, for which they expect some kind of return. Reflecting this change, they are just as likely to give staff time and expertise as a cheque. Progressive companies are paying their staff to help local good causes. The result for the company is improved community relations and the personal development of their employees in terms of skills such as teamwork and communication; the experience also improves staff morale and builds their loyalty to the company.

A poll undertaken for Business in the Community found that cause-related marketing could positively affect consumer perceptions and buying behaviour. The survey revealed that 86 per cent of consumers in Britain were 'more likely to buy a product associated with a cause' when price and quality were the same. For the pioneers of cause-related marketing – companies like The Body Shop, Ben and Jerry's and Traidcraft – business was often as much a vehicle for promoting ethical values, as profits. Cause-related marketing has been criticised by some as the cynical exploitation of vulnerable charities, but charities are not run by gullible people. They are more than capable of negotiating invaluable support without compromising their values or themselves. The power of responsible companies to do good with their big marketing budgets should not be underestimated (see Carphone Warehouse's links with the charity Get Connected described in Chapter 5 of this book). Tesco's Computers for Schools programme, which has been running since 1992, has undoubtedly been good for the company's reputation. But the money has also delivered over £ 62.5 million worth of computing equipment to schools in the UK, the equivalent of one computer for every school.

In 1999, a group of the UK's leading businesses and advocacy groups convened a Committee of Inquiry to revisit the conclusions of the RSA Inquiry. Their report, 'A New Vision for Business', consigned the shareholder versus stakeholder debate to the past.

> It is generally recognised that companies which inspire the engagement not just of their stakeholders but of a wider circle of stakeholders ... can be competitive in the short term and more sustainable in the long term than those which focus exclusively on the financial bottom line. Good business is, by its very nature, responsible business.... There is no fundamental clash between enhanced competitiveness on the one hand and meeting these diverse expectations on the other.

If business is to be trusted to achieve the benefits of globalisation, and to survive as the delivery mechanism for both the wealth and the efficient services our societies require, it has to demonstrate that it is the solution, not the problem.

A UK Committee of Inquiry into some of these issues stated:

> Some have argued that it is only business that can now provide the human, technological and financial resources to meet some of the [world's] problems. Even those who are unnerved at such a prospect (on the grounds of what it means for the health of our democracies and civil institutions) acknowledge that business now has a pivotal role in delivering real improvements in people's lives over and above the goods and services they provide and the profits they generate.

This thought was well expounded by Steve Hilton, a pro-business, pro-stakeholder campaigner writing in the *Guardian* in 2001.

> Free trade and profitable business are the best ways to deliver social progress.... Business has the potential to act as an engine of social change, using its creative thinking, economic resources and cultural power to improve lives.... Conservatives dismiss this as 'adding to the burdens of business'.... They're completely out of step with social trends; a new generation of managers is rising to the top of many leading companies – individuals who are socially concerned and have progressive ideas about what their companies could do to make the world a better place. Not because they're altruists but because they recognise the tremendous economic and cultural power they wield, and want to find creative ways of using that power for good while delivering financial returns.

The challenge for business at the beginning of this century is to demonstrate it deserves the responsibility and better reputation it seeks.

As forces for good in the world, leading stakeholder companies are beginning to earn back public respect for business. But they must become typical, not the exceptions. In the twenty-first century business revolution – the stakeholder/corporate citizenship/corporate social responsibility movement, and its increasing adoption by business – lies a real chance for a better world. We need business and industry to create the wealth to maintain our ever-improving standard of living and quality of life. We need business and industry to provide solutions, not create problems. Business and industry can earn the licence to do business by driving these concepts forward; citizens can help by encouraging them when they do right, as well as criticising what they do wrong.

Above all, those who advocate the cause of private enterprise should understand that if it is to flourish – in particular if it is to be accepted as the best way to improve performance in areas previously seen as the prerogative of the public sector, as some in the UK argue that it should – it must accept the responsibilities that come with that: accountability and a commitment to the highest of values. It should not be beyond a new breed of business leaders to achieve this, and in so doing to show that shareholder value and stakeholder value are not alternatives but go hand in hand to the benefit of all.

The words 'big business' have in recent years too often conjured up an image of destructive, uncaring corporate profiteering and of personal greed. As an image of business this is of course crude and unfair, based partly on extremes of bad corporate behaviour and partly on the exploitation by the more irresponsible or ideological campaigners of the popular media's tendency to over-simplify and portray a word of goodies and baddies with little in between. Many good and caring people in business simply do not recognise this image and rightly resent it, but no image is completely undeserved. There has been bad corporate behaviour. There has been a failure to accept the rights of stakeholders. Now, at the beginning of the twenty-first century, we stand at a moment of opportunity, for an idea has emerged, its value has been proved, and experience exists to build upon. The best must give a lead in encouraging best behaviour and in promoting change. The twenty-first century revolution must become better known and must be driven onwards and upwards, for it is as important as those that went before it.

Part II
BAA
A Case History

CHAPTER 3

Contract With the Community
How BAA Found a Way to Live With its Neighbours

David Grayson, the corporate citizenship guru from Business in the Community, in a foreword to this book, emphasises the pace of change. 'A single day's growth in the US economy today is equal to the entire year's worth in 1830', he claims. 'The equivalent of all the science done in 1960 happens in one day today. All of the foreign exchange dealings around the world in 1979 would be performed in a day today, as would all the telephone calls made around the world in 1984. In one day now, as many e-mails are sent around the world as in the whole of 1989.' And so on.

One monumental change over the past 100 years has been in the number of people who fly. It was in 1903 that the Wright brothers gave the human race powered flight. The first commercial flight from Heathrow took place in 1946. Rather over 50 years later, prior to the terrorist attacks on New York and Washington in September 2001 and the responses to them, UK airports alone handled more than 170 million passengers a year, a number which was expected to rise to over 333 million by 2015.

We all want to fly: to holiday overseas, to explore the world, to visit family and friends who live abroad, to participate in international cultural, sport and political events, and to generally broaden our life experiences. We also travel on business, of course. And it is not just a question of 'wanting' to fly; a much higher proportion of the population can now afford to travel more widely and more often, and they are doing so. For many, the entire planet is now as accessible as a neighbouring county was a century ago and, despite recent troubles and turmoil, it is hard to believe that there will in the longer term be any going back on this.

The pace of change is underlined by a 1999 UK survey conducted for BAA in which 85 per cent of people said they had flown, compared with 61 per cent of their parents and 29 per cent of their grandparents. Air travel has become an inherent part of modern life. And, of course, the phenomenon is world-wide. In the year 2000, over 1.65 billion people around the world chose to fly. By 2015, the number is expected to double. The world is a smaller place as a result. And it is a richer place: the aviation industry is one of the great engines of economic growth. For instance, it underpins the world's number one industry, tourism: an industry that has not only enhanced our quality of life, but is vital to the well-being of many poorer countries. It is a major industry for developed countries too, contributing over £60 billion to the UK alone; you only have to observe the devastation to the rural economy caused by the impact on tourism of foot and mouth disease in 2001 to catch a glimpse of its importance to the country. Likewise the (we believe temporary) huge setback to the industry after the September terrorist attacks underlined its importance to the wider economy.

'The Economic Impact of Aviation in the UK', a report published in 1999 by Oxford Economic Forecasting (OEF) and financed jointly by the DETR and the industry, quantifies the aviation industry's contribution to the UK economy. Starting with employment, it says the industry:

- employs 180 000 people directly
- creates employment for 200 000 people indirectly through the supply chain
- maintains 75 000 jobs in travel agencies
- supports 100 000 jobs in the wider economy through the spending of employees in the aviation, supply and travel industries.

It estimates that by 2015 the total number of employees in the UK economy dependent on aviation will have risen to around 700 000.

The OEF report finds aviation to be a key catalyst for other growth industries, underpinning wider business success and driving UK competitiveness. As well as tourism, the 'knowledge-based' industries, such as pharmaceuticals, computers, software, electronics and other communications industries rely heavily on UK aviation to give them swift and direct access to global markets.

It warns that there are potentially serious economic penalties for Britain if the expected growth in aviation is curtailed. OEF estimates that if the forecast growth in passenger numbers is restricted by 25 million passengers, by 2015, the UK would have 36 000 fewer jobs, 0.6 per cent a year less investment and £4 billion a year less GDP than would be the case if there were no restrictions.

BAA airports alone employ over 110 000 people directly, and Heathrow itself is responsible for approximately 66 500 direct jobs. A study commissioned by BAA from DTZ Pieda Consulting supported the OEF report in finding that airports have three other direct employment impacts: direct off-airport employment, indirect employment (supported by purchases of goods and services by firms engaged on- and off-airport) and induced employment (supported by local expenditures of persons employed directly and indirectly). A similar independent study, commissioned by BAA Scottish Airports and undertaken by the Fraser of Allander Institute in 1997, showed that Glasgow, Edinburgh and Aberdeen airports are significant generators of wealth. Directly and indirectly, they contribute £ 1.3 billion to the Scottish economy, with Glasgow Airport accounting for almost £ 600 million, Edinburgh making up £ 300 million and Aberdeen contributing almost £ 400 million.

Given the above, it is not surprising that there is intense competition between European capitals for international aviation business. London is the leading aviation hub in the world, with both the largest (Heathrow), and the sixth-largest (Gatwick) international airports, as well as Stansted and the two smaller airports, Luton and City. The UK capital owes its success as an aviation hub to the millions of passengers who use Heathrow, and increasingly Gatwick, to connect to other flights. More than 90 airlines fly to over 160 destinations in 85 countries from Heathrow alone. It is not often appreciated that a third of the airport's passengers never leave its terminals; they just fly in and then out, connecting to other flights in London, but still contributing £ 1 billion a year to the UK economy while they do so. These connecting passengers also help to support less busy routes where point-to-point traffic would not be economic, thus widening the travel options for UK people. Its role of top international hub is keenly sought by rival European cities, notably Paris, Frankfurt and Amsterdam, all of which are investing heavily to expand the terminal and runway capacity of their airports. Paris, for example, is in the midst of a £ 4.5 billion programme, including the construction of two new terminals and runways that will increase the capacity of Charles de Gaulle and Orly Airports to 60 million by 2004.

Access to international flights is a key factor when foreign investors decide where to put their money. London is ranked number one among Europe's cities for its international air links, and it is no coincidence that the UK attracts more inward investors than any other country in the EU. One-third of Europe's top 1000 companies have their headquarters in London, more than twice the number in any other EU country.

This brings us to the issue facing BAA in the early 1990s. Before it was privatised in 1987, BAA plc had been the British Airports Authority (people often still call it that, but it ceased to be so 15 years back). Since it was privatised the company has invested heavily in developing Heathrow and Gatwick and building Stansted. In the early 1990s, it anticipated that by 2015 demand for London's airports would double to more than 184 million passengers per year. It also anticipated that the combined runway capacity of 176 million would fall short of that demand; by 2015, the south-east would have completely run out of runway capacity. So plans had to be made for further expansion, not just because the company wanted to grow for its own business reasons but because it was obliged to grow; that is what national airports policy expected of it, and that is what its regulator, the CAA, encouraged by anxious airlines, was insisting that it should do.

But grow where? Heathrow had additional runway capacity (that is, it could handle more planes on its two runways), but it could not utilise this fully because its terminals and aircraft parking spaces were becoming full. Gatwick had spare runway capacity, but the chances of expanding beyond this with a second runway were not good, at least not until 2019 because BAA had entered into a legally-binding agreement with West Sussex County Council not to seek another runway at the airport before then. As for Stansted, it had the capacity to grow significantly, but even realising the full capacity of its runway would leave a deficit across the south-east as a whole.

One thing was clear: in the circumstances, leaving valuable runway capacity at Heathrow unused made no sense, not just to the company but to its airline customers and, indeed, to the nation, whose main gateways were in danger of becoming blocked. BAA decided, therefore, to seek planning permission for a fifth terminal (T5) at Heathrow, not to increase the capacity of the airport but to *realise* the capacity of its runways to handle the traffic.

The case appeared overwhelming. Without T5 there would be a major crisis of supply. Furthermore, the terminal would be a beautiful building, the first spectacular British construction of the twenty-first century, a structure of glass and steel with sweeping panoramas, a national gateway for the twenty-first century of which Britain could be proud. And its local environmental impact would be relatively minimal. Normally with large aviation construction projects, rows of houses are compulsorily purchased and torn down, but the site for T5 was a sludge works between Heathrow's two runways within the boundaries of the airport. There was no other use to which the land could be put.

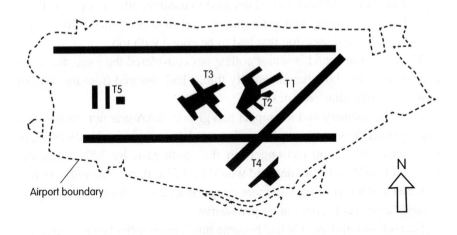

Figure 3.1 Terminal 5 Heathrow
This shows how T5 fits within the perimeters of the airport between the two runways. No other human activity could take place there

BAA unveiled its vision for T5 in May 1992, knowing that the new terminal would be the subject of a Public Inquiry. The company was confident; it had a powerful case based on national aviation policy requiring it to meet demand when and where it arose, and it was operating within a planning process which in the previous two decades had delivered permissions for the growth of all three BAA London airports (Terminal 4 at Heathrow, Gatwick's North Terminal, and a new terminal – but in its capacity effectively a new airport – at Stansted).

So, yes, the company was confident, but there was, it has to be admitted, also an element of complacency. Many company veterans argued that BAA had always won permission for every expansion it had needed, so why worry about getting permission for T5? Of course it would win. Like many in other industries, they had not fully considered the changes that had been taking place in the world around them, changes that became only too clear to John Egan when he was confronted by local people in the Richmond Theatre in 1994 and felt the extent of their concern.

John had known, of course, of the local anxieties about further growth at Heathrow, but that night he was struck by the depth and strength of feeling. He became more disconcerted when he realised that nearly all

Heathrow's local authorities had decided to band together to oppose T5. It was clear the company had more than a legal fight on its hands; there was a whole political dimension that had to be coped with too.

The more John and his senior colleagues considered the issue, the more they realised just how fundamentally things had changed from the days of those early planning victories.

First, the industry and its impact had grown; BAA was not starting this inquiry from the same place. When Terminal 4 was approved in 1979, there were only 39 million passengers in the south-east; by 2001 when the decision would be taken, demand would be 115 million. The industry had a greater and wider impact on more people than ever before; the 'enough is enough' case had become more persuasive.

Second, ordinary people had become much more articulate and effective at fighting their corner. A better-educated population was no longer prepared to be bypassed; it expected its concerns to be heard and addressed. At national level major companies were being forced to respond to pressure from national consumer and environmental groups on a variety of issues. Most of these groups had a local branch, and there were other local organisations around Heathrow – such as HACAN, the main anti-T5 group – to ensure opponents had a vehicle for protest. Thus when BAA's managers and lawyers finally took their seats at the T5 Public Inquiry on 16 May 1995, they faced a formal coalition of 30 local authorities, councils and anti-noise groups claiming to represent a considerable number of people. The tenacity of this coalition and the determination of the Inspector to ensure the issues it raised were fully explored would turn the T5 Public Inquiry into the longest in British history, probably in world history.

Third, aviation had become a more contentious environmental issue. For the first time environmental groups like Friends of the Earth were asking questions about the impact of increasing passenger demand. Whereas in the past an additional terminal or runway would have been largely a local issue, it was now capable of becoming a national *cause célèbre*, as the damaging protests over the additional runway at Manchester would become testimony. The sustainability of aviation was rising rapidly up the environmental agenda.

At the time Des Wilson joined BAA, it was being recognised that the company had made two mistakes. First, as already mentioned, it had inevitably focused heavily on the technicalities and legal presentation of the case but far too little on the political challenge: it had under-estimated the capacity of Heathrow's neighbours to lengthen the process, to put pressure on the Inquiry and to move it into a wider political context. Second, it was putting too much faith in its old relationship with government transport officials. They were, of course, generally supportive of the policy of meeting demand, but both the company and the officials themselves were failing to recognise that the days when this view would automatically prevail were gone.

The tensions between the old and the new came to a head at a memorable dinner at the Goring Hotel near BAA's Victoria offices in the summer of 1994, when Des Wilson met the BAA team handling the inquiry process for the first time. They explained that the T5 Inquiry was, in effect, more than one inquiry. It would also deal with permissions for a number of road works and other operations associated with the project, including how a terminal access road would connect to the M25. This would coincide with the highly contentious governmental proposals for a widening of the M25 to 14 lanes. While BAA was stressing that this widening to 14 lanes was not needed for T5, the terminal's opponents inevitably chose to publicise it as one of the adverse effects the new terminal would cause.

Des asked why, if the 14 lanes were not needed for T5, the company was supporting the plan. 'Because we've been asked to,' was the reply. He then argued that as the widening of the M25 was one of the three or four major complaints being hammered home in leaflets by T5's opponents, it made little sense for BAA to support a project that was not essential to the airport: 'It's hugely controversial, we don't need it and we're being blamed for it. Why don't we support our neighbours instead?'

So the company withdrew its support for the 14-lane M25. Its position proved a key factor in the 14-lane scheme eventually being ruled out and more restricted widening being concentrated on a few key congestion points. Thus, instead of testifying as opponents to the local community, BAA had become a key agent on their behalf: an advocate of solutions instead of part of the problem.

The company decided to make a fresh start in its approach to the T5 issue, and began by polling local people to establish exactly what they were concerned about. The polls were conducted by Gallup within the noise footprint and a five-mile radius of the airport, and were slightly weighted towards the most affected areas. At the same time company representatives attended scores of local meetings to discuss the proposal and its implications and to listen to local concerns. There were a number of surprises. To begin with, despite the fact that HACAN and other opponents had virtually had the battlefield to themselves because of BAA's concentration on its technical case, more people in the area supported T5 than opposed it. This was, in fact, so surprising to some that the company decided to repeat the poll a few weeks later to check its accuracy. The second poll replicated the findings almost exactly (as further polls were to do over the following few years, the majority in support of T5 actually growing all the time).

There were other interesting findings. The polls showed that people's concerns differed according to where they lived but that, on the whole, aircraft noise was not as important an issue as the company had expected. The major local concerns were:

- the fear that T5 was 'just another step' that would lead to a third runway and an ever-enlarging airport with ever-increasing impacts on local communities
- the fear of increasing traffic on the roads
- the fear of more night flights.

The company began to do two things. First was to seek reassuring answers – *real* answers – to these questions. Second, it sought to communicate that it had been listening and was responding.

The first sign of this change of approach was the letter from John that arrived at 500 000 homes in the Heathrow area on the first morning of the Inquiry. In it he wrote:

> I want to make a firm promise to you, on behalf of the Board of Directors of BAA plc, and on behalf of the management of Heathrow Airport that we will:
> - Address the concerns raised by you, our neighbours.
> - Take practical steps to minimise our impact on the community.
> - Report to you annually on our progress.

The letter reassured members of the local community that:

- T5 does not call for another runway.
- T5 will not lead to a fourteen lane M25.
- T5 will not cause more noise than today.
- T5 will not increase the quota of night flights.

The company began an internal debate into how it should set about keeping its promises to listen and to respond.

The key players included Egan and Wilson, along with Richard Everitt, then BAA's strategy and compliance director – himself a significant progressive influence within the company on these issues, and in his own quiet way, a visionary in the area of corporate responsibility – and Michael Maine, the man then in charge of the T5 case, who had been more exposed than anyone to local feeling. From the start, all were at one on a fundamental principle: the answer could not be a cosmetic one. The company had to make real concessions to local concerns; it had to come up with practical solutions to real problems. As Michael Maine said at the time, 'You can't tell people they can't hear noise when they can, that they can't see cars when they can.... If they're to believe you're acting on these issues you have to achieve a real result.'

This may seem so obvious a conclusion that it should go without saying. But compare it to many companies and industries (such as the lead industry cited in our introductory chapter), who believed they could simply steamroller over people's concerns; compare it with other companies who have tried to placate local communities with a purely cosmetic approach, or tried to cover up their plans until it was too late for the community to influence them; compare it even with some in the aviation industry who took the view that BAA had 'gone soft' and was preparing to make concessions it need never make. Most vocal of the last group was Robert Ayling, then chief executive of British Airways, who, perhaps because he was a lawyer and also a former Whitehall civil servant, believed that BAA should rely on the legal case and Whitehall support, and that every concession should be dragged out of the company only as a last resort.

BAA, however, was changing its approach dramatically, accepting that the world around it had changed and it either had to change with it or come into conflict with it. So the questions were: what are our neighbours' concerns? And how can we address them *in a meaningful way*?

The major concern was that T5 would lead to a third runway at Heathrow. Another runway was, of course, a symbol to the local community of unfettered growth. They rightly pointed out that at earlier public inquiries, such as that for Terminal 4, promises had appeared to be made about no further expansion. The community call was straightforward: 'Enough is enough!'

The timing of the work on Runway Capacity in the South East, a project known as RUCATSE, could not have been worse. Recognising that even after

T5 was built there would still be capacity problems in the south-east, the government was exploring the next step. Inevitably the study considered Heathrow as a possible location for a new runway. There were other options, of course, but its initial report said: 'Heathrow would afford the greatest benefits to the air-transport industry and passengers'. On the other hand, it acknowledged the Heathrow option 'would give rise to the greatest scale of disadvantages in terms of noise impact on people, land use and property demolition'. That was putting it mildly; the illustration in the RUCATSE report presented Heathrow's neighbours with what they regarded as Armageddon: positioned between the A4 and M4 to the north of the airport, the third parallel runway would wipe out 3300 houses in three villages.

The anti-T5 campaigners seized the report as proof there was more to the new terminal than BAA was letting on; that T5 was 'a Trojan horse'. Once again, BAA refuted the claim: 'T5 is about realising the capacity of Heathrow's existing runways; it has nothing to do with a new runway', the company said. It expressed its own scepticism about the practicality of another runway. The phrase, repeated over and over, was that in the company's view it was 'a political and environmental non-runner'.

The doubt had been raised, however. The company's polls showed that 70 per cent of local people believed T5 would lead to a third runway. Furthermore – and this, alas, was a reflection of the company's more cavalier approach to the local community in earlier years – people simply did not believe what BAA was now saying. Nor was the position helped by the fact that British Airways took the view that there should be a third runway at Heathrow and, while frequently urged to accept the political realities, could not be persuaded from, at least privately, making its views clear.

BAA had one other problem; the decision was not in its hands. Deciding on the siting of runways and where growth could and could not take place was the prerogative of Whitehall. BAA could however make its views known, and it now took a crucial decision: to ask for a third runway at Heathrow to be ruled out. Following the M25 widening initiative, it was for the second time positioning itself as an advocate on the side of the local community.

A local newspaper reported John's commitment:

I have made it quite clear to the local community that BAA has no plans or proposals for an additional runway at Heathrow. The environmental impact of that proposal would be such that we do not believe that permission could be granted under the existing planning system. The Government must now move swiftly to put local residents' minds at rest by ruling out this option.

The government responded. On 2 February 1995, it announced:

> The Government has concluded that while RUCATSE's analysis showed a strong case for additional runway capacity in the south-east, the RUCATSE options for a third runway at Heathrow or a second runway at Gatwick should not be considered further.

BAA then decided to put the issue beyond doubt by making its view on a third runway clear at the Inquiry. In a letter to the Inquiry's Inspector, the company's leading Inquiry barrister, Lord Silsoe said:

> It is the company's view that the local communities around Heathrow should be given assurances.... BAA would urge the Government to rule out any additional runway at Heathrow, and BAA would support a recommendation by the Inquiry Inspector in his report that the Government should rule it out. Indeed BAA invites the Inspector to make such a recommendation.

This was a big moment. This was a request from the airport operator itself that the main factor in the growth of an airport and therefore its own business – its ability to add to its runways – be ruled out. (As we have said, the company's problem was that the decision was not within its own power; thus it had to represent its position as a request or a point of view; but, be in no doubt, this was a highly influential point of view being presented by the main player in any such debate.)

If you look back at all the HACAN and other leaflets being published in the local community in 1994 before the Inquiry began, you will find two main threats high-lighted: a 14-lane M25 and a third runway. The first was now definitely ruled out; the second, as a result of BAA's position, probably would be too. On two of the community's biggest issues the company had listened and responded, siding with the community on both.

These, however, were issues that could be addressed by a simple change of policy – if you like, by the stroke of a pen. The other issues required more practical and/or far more expensive measures.

The first was aircraft noise. Many local residents who remember the ear-splitting roar of the first jets at the airport acknowledge that there have been significant improvements in noise levels. Since the early 1960s, technological advances have reduced annoyance from noise during take-off and landing by 75 per cent. An Airbus A-320 has an intrusive noise footprint of 1.5 square kilometres on takeoff, compared with the 14 square kilometres of the older Boeing 727. The Boeing 777 carries almost the same number of passengers as the early 747s, but makes barely half the noise.

Despite these improvements, aircraft noise is still a nuisance. The issue manifests itself at a local level, but affects communities the world over. In 1995 the White House Science and Technology Council threw its weight behind local communities by challenging the aviation industry 'to reduce the perceived noise levels of future aircraft by a factor of two from today's subsonic aircraft within 10 years, and by a factor of four within 20 years'.

Today the challenge is being taken forward by ambitious research projects on both sides of the Atlantic. In the US, NASA's Quiet Aircraft Technology Programme is researching how to decrease noise from engines and airframes and to develop operating procedures that will reduce aircraft noise footprints. And in Europe, the EU Silencer (R) enlisted 51 companies in similar research. The European target is to validate new technologies for reducing aircraft noise by six decibels by 2008. These and related programmes are costing hundreds of millions of pounds, reflecting the competitive advantage which quieter aircraft now bring to manufacturers.

Reflecting this trend, the International Civil Aviation Organisation (ICAO), the UN body responsible for regulating international aviation, has banned all of the noisiest aircraft (termed 'Chapter 2') from April 2002. To differentiate the best from the worst performers in the quieter 'Chapter 3' category, it has announced standards for an even more stringent noise rating, 'Chapter 4', for 2006.

BAA cannot, of course, control aircraft noise, but the company does not think the industry has gone far enough and has itself called for a further four decibels improvement, which would make a total reduction of 14 decibels. It has sought to fight the community corner in other ways as well, for technology is not the only way to help give local residents a quieter life; it also calls for care and discipline by the airlines. BAA fines aircraft which exceed noise limits and spends the funds on local good causes; the company has erected noise walls to shield local communities from ground noise and, in partnership with Air Traffic Control and the airlines, it is improving the percentage of aircraft on track around the most populated areas, and using the quieter continuous descent approach, which reduces the surge from aircraft engines on landing.

At Heathrow, the trend towards quieter aircraft and technology has reduced the number of people annoyed by aircraft noise (the so-called 57 LEQ footprint) from 2 092 000 in 1972 to 331 000 in 1999 (the latest year for which figures are available), despite the number of flights almost doubling. Back in 1994, before the T5 Inquiry, BAA assessed that when T5 became operational, the overall noise climate around Heathrow would be no worse than for that particular year. It was so confident about this that it eventually became the first major airport company in the world to propose what would in effect be a noise cap – at that 1994 level.

A noise-related issue that the company found harder to address was that of night flights. Scheduled from 4.55 am (2001), predominantly from the Far East and US, early-morning arrivals are probably Heathrow's most contentious local issue. Inevitably, opponents of T5 were strident in their claims that T5 would mean an increase in the number of night flights. In fact it was BAA's case that the new terminal would actually relieve pressure for early-morning arrivals. A number of flights are scheduled to arrive early because of a shortage of aircraft parking bays (stands) in the morning peak. By increasing the number of stands, T5 would make this unnecessary. Once more, the decision on this was not for BAA; Whitehall decides the limits on night flights. But once more the company put itself on the line, asking the Inquiry in effect to rule out an increase in the quota of night flights.

This left one other major local concern to resolve: road traffic. Ironically, surface traffic caused more distress to local people than air traffic. BAA argued that a third of Heathrow's non-connecting passengers were already using public transport to get to and from the airport (a higher figure than for any other major airport in the world), and that T5 would mean just 3 per cent more vehicles on local roads at peak times, bringing the airport's proportion of total vehicles to just 17 per cent at peak times. But the company still shared the concerns of local people; after all, gridlock on local roads would severely hamper Heathrow's operations.

BAA decided to take a three-part approach:

1. To encourage the use of public transport
2. To discourage car users
3. To persuade the 68 000 people who work at Heathrow not to come by road.

At the heart of this approach was an ambitious long term vision of 50 per cent of Heathrow's passengers using public transport. It would rely on a combination of measures, not all of them controlled directly by BAA, but on this issue the company put its own money on the table: no less than £620 million to cover a brand-new railway service, the Heathrow Express, together with the extension of the Piccadilly Line to T5, and a range of other initiatives and services.

BAA told the inquiry that it wanted Heathrow to become one of the world's best examples of integrated transport, with T5 as its centrepiece. Specifically designed as a fully integrated transport hub, it would allow passengers to pass easily between air, rail, bus, coach and car in one place: a truly world-class air and surface transport interchange. And by extending the Heathrow Express track and tunnels to the west, via T5, BAA would increase Heathrow's rail capacity from 10 to 16 trains an hour each way, creating opportunities to put the airport at the heart of the national rail network.

To offer additional reassurance that the road traffic impact of the new terminal would be no worse than its predictions, BAA volunteered to cap car park spaces under its control at 46 000, the level needed with T5 in 2015.

The T5 Public Inquiry lasted nearly four years. While the authors of this book may be assumed to be biased, most neutral observers acknowledged that BAA's case was never seriously dented, and that demand for T5 was established; that there were no alternatives. Furthermore, the company's concessions on the major issues were welcomed. By the time the inquiry ended on 17 March 1999, BAA was presenting the local community with what it called 'the T5 bargain', formulated partly in terms of proposed conditions, partly in terms of action beyond the inquiry (such as the transport area).

On the negative side was an 8 per cent increase in flights and a 3 per cent increase in road traffic at peak times. But there was also good news: conditions proposed to the Inspector by BAA would, if accepted, rule out a third runway, and create what would in effect be caps on noise, night flights and parking. In fact, what was offered at the Inquiry included no fewer than 500 detailed concessions to the concerns raised by the local community. And there would be £ 620 million worth of public transport initiatives.

On the last day of the Inquiry John Egan wrote back to the 500 000 households he had contacted on the opening day:

> I'm pleased to confirm that we have kept our word. Every specific pledge we made in that letter has been repeated formally to the Inquiry; every practical step has been taken. T5:
>
> - Won't lead to more overall noise – We are prepared to be legally bound to ensure that the area affected by aircraft noise will be kept below what it was in 1994. This is possible because aircraft are getting quieter.
> - Won't lead to a huge increase in the number of planes – While the terminal will handle around 60 per cent more passengers, the increase in flights will be around 8 per cent. This is because, as well as getting quieter, the average aircraft at Heathrow is carrying more passengers.
> - Won't lead to an increase in the night flight quota – We have invited the Inquiry inspector to recommend this to the government.
> - Won't change the way the airport operates – We recognise the community places a high value on runway alternation and have told both the Inquiry and the House of Commons Transport Select Committee that Terminal Five does not require a change in the current system of single runway operation, i.e. it does not need mixed mode where take-offs and landings are being conducted on both runways at the same time.
> - Won't lead to a huge increase in road traffic – Just as there will be more planes, there will be more cars, but only 3 per cent more at peak times throughout the area. In addition, we have offered a cap on car park spaces under our control, so that the number will never exceed what is predicted with Terminal Five.
> - Will lead to an increase in rail capacity – Terminal Five creates an opportunity to increase Heathrow's rail capacity from 10 to 16 trains an hour each way.

It had, Des Wilson argued in a speech in London, been an unnecessarily lengthy and expensive exercise, but in terms of the debate and the concessions 'it was the democratic system producing a real result for all those involved'.

The local community appeared to agree. Gallup were asked to conduct yet another poll to establish the effect of these assurances on local opinion. They asked: 'If all of these conditions were to be met, would you support the building of a new terminal at Heathrow or not?' Sixty per cent of those polled said yes, and 29 per cent no, nearly a two-to-one majority of people who had a view.

The Gallup poll was the latest of seven opinion polls conducted during the course of the Inquiry. Each one showed not only a significant majority in support of the terminal, but one that grew as the concessions were made (see Figure 3.2). The company had been reasonable, and now Heathrow's neighbours were responding; they had legitimate concerns, but once satisfied that these were being addressed they were prepared to accept Terminal Five. Much later, in late 2000, BAA polled the local community once more, and the support was holding up: 60 per cent again. In 2001 it decided to change polling companies to see if another company would replicate the findings. In June it got a positive answer, a 59 to 24 vote in support of the terminal. Just as significant, 69 per cent said they had a broadly positive view of Heathrow, further evidence that the airport's opponents were not representative (only 7 per cent had a negative view of the airport).

This is not the place to make the full case for T5, or to comment on a planning system that led to a project first planned around 1990 being opened (with luck) in 2007. Suffice it to say that both the authors believe the case for T5 was overwhelming and that the 'T5 bargain' emerging from the Inquiry was a reasonable one. What we really want to stress here is that if a company, or any other institution, in either the public or private sector, these days wishes to promote a project that impacts on the local community, it has to be accountable to that community: to say what it is planning, to engage in debate, to listen to concerns and to address them.

As we will discover when we come to discuss Gatwick (in particular) and Stansted, an even better approach to T5 would have been to interface with the local community much earlier and in an open and sharing way. There would still have been opponents, and there would still have been a public inquiry. But the opponents would have been fewer and the inquiry shorter.

In October 2001, some 15 years after the company first began to plan T5, seven years after it published its Statement of Case, six and a half years after the beginning of the public inquiry, two and a half years after the end of the inquiry, and nearly a year after the Inspector submitted his report, the Secretary of State for Transport, Stephen Byers, announced his decision. T5 was approved. Byers told the House of Commons that the development was in the national interest.

> The Inspector stresses in his report that the issue is essentially one of striking a balance. He identifies the benefits of T5. They are considerable. He sees Heathrow as essential for keeping the UK air transport industry strong and competitive … [and] sees wider benefits for London and the UK as a whole. He says Heathrow has done a lot to attract investment to the UK and that London's success as a world city and financial centre would be threatened unless Heathrow remains competitive…. By ensuring Heathrow's success T5 would make a major contribution to the national economy. And he says it would be good for passengers, providing a terminal equal to the best in the world…. I also agree with the Inspector that the real beneficiaries if T5 is not provided will be Charles de Gaulle in Paris, Schipol Amsterdam, and Frankfurt Airport.

In a crucial section of his speech Byers said that:

> The Inspector weighs all the benefits and costs very carefully. He says – and I use his words – that he has come to the clear conclusion that the benefits of Terminal Five would substantially out-weigh the environmental impact as long as the effects are properly controlled.

He then listed a number of conditions including: a limit on flights to 480 000 a year, suggesting a capacity of 90 million passengers a year; a limit on the area most affected by noise; the extension of both the Heathrow Express and the Piccadilly line to T5; and a cap on car parking at a lower level than BAA had asked for. The number of permitted night flights would be further considered.

Thus, of the three main points the company had made to the community, two were addressed: more public transport and controls on car parking to cut back traffic congestion, and controls on noise. The Secretary of State did not respond to the third: BAA's urging at the public inquiry that he should re-assure the community on the third runway issue, but the cap on

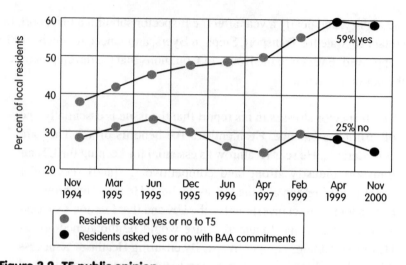

Figure 3.2 T5 public opinion
The chart traces support for T5 over a six-year period, growing as the company's responses to community concerns became clear

flights would appear to make a third runway at Heathrow unnecessary (and we believe it would be both environmentally and politically a non-runner).

Were the opponents satisfied? Of course not: at least, not those who had decided to make opposing T5 their life's cause. Even some of the more sensible opponents, who knew the community had made a considerable gain, were not going to welcome the outcome openly. The overall reaction, however, including that in the local community, was that while the process had been lengthy almost beyond the endurance of the company and the community (and for that matter the country, for it would have to wait another six or seven years before Heathrow could comfortably handle demand), a well-balanced result had emerged.

The Conservative opposition did not criticise the basic decision to proceed with T5, and the newspapers were unanimous in welcoming it. Even the *Guardian*, most reflective of environmental opinion, said it was 'broadly right'. *The Times* said the lengthy inquiry had 'finally reached the right conclusion'. After detailing the tough conditions, it said that Byers:

> could have reminded opponents that buyers have long known that
> houses in the area are subject to aircraft noise – the main reason,

indeed, why prices are cheaper than elsewhere. He could have pointed out that the environmental costs of building a new airport ... are far, far higher than those of a new terminal. And he could have detailed the economic damage suffered by those cities that have trailed in the race to develop new infrastructure and transport links.

The *Daily Telegraph* also called the decision 'a welcome one'. The *Independent* concluded the UK could not have afforded to act in 'virtuous isolation' by allowing all the economic benefits of aviation growth to go elsewhere.

The company was getting its terminal at a price, and that price was, first, to accept that a long-term limit was emerging over its ability to grow this particular airport and, second, to be required to address at considerable financial cost the concerns of one of its key stakeholders: the community.

What mattered to BAA, however, was that it had the terminal it and the nation needed, that it had won respect for the way it had responded to the issues, and that it had learned from the whole experience in a way that would help it in other areas.

Never again would it take the community for granted.

BAA had learned a better way to live with its neighbours.

Contract with the Community

While all this was happening Des Wilson, supported wholeheartedly by John Egan and Richard Everitt, had been developing a plan to build the approach adopted at Heathrow into BAA's philosophy and practices, effectively locking the company into a stakeholder approach. Des launched the proposal at the annual meeting of the company's top 150 managers in late 1995, advocating a progressive approach to corporate citizenship, the adoption of an open, expansion-by-negotiation approach to planning, and a commitment to sustainable growth.

He called the programme 'Contract with the Community'. In a nutshell, the company would ask for permission from its neighbours to develop its airports, in return for sharing their concerns about the negative effects and coming up with practical solutions. Where the negative could not be entirely balanced, the company would compensate its neighbours for the downside by a positive contribution to community life.

Chris Hoare, a long-time BAA manager who was appointed to head the programme, recalls some initial cynicism.

It's fair to say that some managers, particularly those whose roles didn't bring them into contact with local communities, regarded community relations as a kind of penance to be endured by their unfortunate colleagues while they got on with making the money.

In recognition that attitudes can take years to change, Contract with the Community was launched initially as a pragmatic programme geared to the areas where the company's growth aspirations were, and to what it could deliver at any particular time. Cynics would say that the company was therefore doing little more than what it had to do to expand. But Des Wilson was concerned to carry the whole of BAA with him. He well remembered a few years earlier attending a management conference of one of the world's largest companies and hearing a top international board director extolling a corporate-citizen approach, only to be openly attacked by his middle managers who argued that they had enough problems meeting the board's bottom-line objectives without being stuck with this 'do-gooder stuff'.

Des was determined to make the business case for corporate citizenship, and allow the other arguments for it to emerge later. Only by linking the programme to business objectives could he guarantee the budgets and, above all, the managers' commitment.

'You have to remember', he told Chris Hoare and other colleagues, 'that we've studied this approach, we're now educated in its virtues. For many in this company this is completely new thinking. Don't force it. Link it to their current objectives and let it win its own friends.'

A Contract with the Community Board was set up, and to give it greater credibility within the company than if it were, say, public-affairs owned, it was headed by an experienced airport manager, Janis Kong, the tough Managing Director of Gatwick. Representatives were chosen from each sector of the company. A programme of objectives was set, and an educational campaign launched.

The board was only too aware that this was a message that had to be taken to every corner of the company. Workshops were held for managers, and Contract with the Community was built into every staff conference. The board recognised that leadership had to come from the top and a commitment to the Contract was contained in every internal speech John Egan made.

An early step was to set up the company's own charity. BAA's charitable giving had lacked focus and coherence. Airport donations were small and spread thinly; corporate donations were large, but went to national causes with little presence or relevance in airport communities. A review concluded that BAA's charitable giving was providing little benefit in the geographical areas where its business had the greatest impact. It also revealed that the level of the company's giving put it in the second tier of corporate givers.

BAA took decisive action to address these points, increasing its charitable giving by 50 per cent and creating and registering as a charity its Twenty-First Century Communities Trust, to channel donations to specific causes in its airport communities. Though the airports maintained discretionary funds for worthy causes, the Trust focused support on just three areas, 'the three Es':

- **Environment**: helping local groups nurture the physical environment beyond its airports.
- **Education**: assisting projects for the educational and personal development of young people. Support is focused on key areas in the government's national agenda, including leadership management and raising standards in schools.
- **Employment**: helping to develop employment opportunities for local people as well as a significant range of training and recruitment initiatives.

The 'three Es' policy brought new rigour and coherence to the company's charitable donations and community support activities such as employee involvement.

In addition to the local projects the company decided to support one major national project each year. Building on the London Heathrow Youth Games, which it had been supporting for years, it developed the idea of the 'BAA Millennium Youth Games', a spectacular national event involving 250 000 young people in regional heats, culminating in national finals in Southampton in the year 2000.

This support for local community activity mattered; it was the company saying: 'We belong here, many of our employees live here, your problems are our problems.' It was also a way of saying: 'OK, we're not the easiest of neighbours, but we want to be good neighbours and this is a positive thing we can do.'

Of course, it was not nearly enough. The community support programme was to be but one part of the Contract. What really mattered was the way BAA responded to the bigger concerns, and to this end John took the radical step of rewriting the company's mission statement.

For John a mission statement is not just words; it is the company's compass, its route map. It must be extraordinarily precise, saying exactly what the company aims to do, and laying down the way it is going to do it. When any major question about company objectives arose, John would always urge colleagues: 'Go back to the mission statement'.

So changing it was a big decision. The company's aim continued to be the most successful airports group in the world, but with a telling addition – achieving its aim was now conditional on BAA growing 'with the trust and support of its neighbours'.

Another major meeting of the company's top managers was called, and this one had only one subject: Contract with the Community. The company's mission statement had been changed; now everyone had to understand why. John was candid:

> To deny that our neighbours have a genuine stake in the company is to deny not only the reality of their lives, but also their ability to obstruct, delay and even stop the growth of our airports. Our new approach to community relations may well be the right way to behave anyway, but it is also good business.

Des addressed the remaining doubters:

> You may have seen T4 approved in 93 days; Gatwick North approved in 75 days; Stansted – a whole new airport – approved in 265 days. But what about T5's four years? You may believe the old ways will deliver what we want in the end, but I doubt it. And at what cost? It makes adversaries of people who should be our natural allies – our neighbours.

The Contract Board now began embedding the mission into everything the company did. This involved a fundamental programme of culture change in which environmental, social and economic factors were integrated into BAA's decisions, reflected in its objectives, targets, key performance indicators and relationships with its stakeholders.

The ten key principles underlying Contract with the Community were published for all to see. They have been developed over the years and now stand as follows:

We will:

1. Promote a vision for cleaner, smarter growth in aviation which maximises the positive benefits for society – facilitating prosperity, regeneration, regional and UK competitiveness, cultural exchange and social inclusion – while minimising negative social and environmental impacts.
2. Pursue a stakeholder partnership approach to the decision-making process on new developments and other issues affecting the wider community, listening to and understanding the concerns of stakeholders, and developing practical programmes of action to address them.
3. Integrate strategies, incentives and reward systems to ensure that sustainable development priorities are reflected in day-to-day decisions and operations at each of our airports.
4. Improve performance through objectives, externally audited targets, key performance indicators and by reflecting these priorities in relationships with business partners and suppliers.
5. Influence solutions for wider environmental improvements and aviation's contribution to climate change directly through the industry as well as government and bodies such as Airports Council International and the UN International Civil Aviation Organisation.
6. Proactively engage in global, EU and national government consultations on the sustainable development of the aviation industry.
7. Act responsibly as a corporate citizen and employer.
8. Think long-term and seek to be challenged by leading experts.
9. Communicate our performance within the company and externally via a process of integrated annual sustainable development reporting supported by annual external audit and verification.
10. Explore the environmental and financial gains to be secured through innovation and technology.

In 1998, BAA reported its environmental, social and economic performance in its first sustainability report. This addressed the company's
neighbours and other stakeholders in the same way as its annual report and
accounts addressed its shareholders. To underline the point, the company
became the first to publish its sustainability and annual financial reports
side-by-side on the day of its financial results, and to have the sustainability
claims independently audited. (Later the two reports were to be integrated
to further stress the comparable importance of the issues.)

The approach won BAA the award for Best Site Reporter in the prestigious Association of Chartered and Certified Accountants (ACCA)
Environmental Reporting Awards. The award recognised BAA's 'fully-
developed site reporting package' of individual airport reports charting
progress against specific environmental targets and objectives, all in the
context of an overall corporate report. The judges were also impressed with
the community focus of the BAA reports.

In 1999, the following year, BAA's sustainability reporting expanded in
line with the principles of the Global Reporting Initiative and now included
its performance as an employer. The company's progressive approach was
recognised by ACCA with another top environmental award. This time,
BAA was joint runner-up overall. Once again, the company's approach to
community reporting was singled out for praise by the judges.

In 2000, the company received the ultimate accolade when it achieved the
highest score of 50 leading international companies surveyed on their
sustainability reporting record. The Global Reporters survey was undertaken
by the UN Environment Programme and SustainAbility, the world-renowned
think-tank committed to encouraging sustainable principles in business and
the highest standards of accountability.

Managing sustainability issues is now considered to be a core competency
for BAA's senior managers; if they have not got this ability, the opportunities
for their advancement within the company are limited. Competency in this
area is assessed within the broader BAA management competency framework, a 360-degree profiler in which individual managers, their direct
reports, their own managers and other colleagues to appraise their performance. The company's environmental performance is now part of the senior
management incentive scheme. If annual environmental targets are not met,
managers do not get their full bonus. Their personal targets (which align
directly with the new BAA mission) now include a contribution to 'growing
with the support and trust of our neighbours'. They are appraised on the

extent to which they have met these targets through a process that includes external verification, and the result is reflected in their bonuses.

In 1999, BAA set five challenging medium/long-term environmental objectives for the business as a whole in areas identified as of greatest concern to its national and local stakeholders: climate change, local air quality, noise, surface transport and waste. The objectives are designed to mitigate the impact of its business activities on the environment and, where appropriate, align with UK national and regional objectives for sustainable development.

The company also developed a Strategic Airport Planning Process, which provides early practical advice to those shaping airport develop-ment proposals about the likely scale of environmental and local community impacts, possible mitigation measures and the costs of failing to implement them.

Each business unit within BAA sets its annual objectives on the basis of a balanced scorecard: an assessment of how it is contributing to the company's mission, including the need to grow with the trust and support of its neighbours.

In addition, every airport has its own Contract with the Community (sometimes simply referred to as its sustainable development programme), covering how it is contributing to government, regional and local agendas for sustainable development, and involving its stakeholders in key deci-sions. The Contract is also the framework document for setting local targets that deliver real improvements in performance.

Cross-functional boards and committees, some championed by a board director or airport managing director, are supporting the integration of sustainable development within BAA. Through cross-functional initiatives coordinated by these boards, the company is engaging every part of the airport business – from airport planning and procurement, to front-line operations – in Contract with the Community.

Growing Gatwick

The first big test of the ability of BAA's new mission statement to deliver business results was at Gatwick, where passengers were set to rise from 30 million to around 40 million per annum by 2008. The airport had to expand to accommodate them. It needed a bigger and better international departures lounge, check-in areas, stands and taxiways, baggage reclaim halls and baggage facilities – an investment of close to £ 1 billion within its two terminal, one runway configuration.

As company managers contemplated the planning consents they would need, one thing was foremost in their minds. 'I thought of the four-year T5 Inquiry and said: "let's not do it that way"', says Janis Kong, the airport's Managing Director.

In fact, if there were a better way, BAA did not want to go through a public inquiry at Gatwick at all. In previous large developments like T5, the company had effectively decided exactly what it wanted, developed its plans in minute detail, announced them, and defended them in a public inquiry. This was the traditional planning process: adversarial, at times unpleasant, and resulting in planning permission for the development with legally-binding planning conditions to mitigate its impact. Everyone won something, but because of the time, expense, stress and damaged relationships of the process, everyone lost as well – except, of course, for the lawyers.

If planning conditions were inevitable, BAA reasoned, why not turn the whole process on its head and make them up front? So it did at Gatwick what it wished it had done at Heathrow: it side-stepped the lawyers and asked those affected by Gatwick's operations – local authorities, residents, environmental and other interest groups – how Gatwick could grow in a way that was acceptable to them and what assurances they would need to agree to it.

In spring 1999, before the company tabled any planning applications, and indeed before its plans were fully formed, it launched its biggest-ever consultation exercise, circulating draft development, environment, employment and transport strategies to Gatwick's neighbouring local authorities in East and West Sussex and Surrey, as well as individuals, business and community groups in the local community.

The company had face-to-face meetings with local planners, officers and members, not just from the local planning authorities of Crawley Borough Council and West Sussex County Council, but all the local councils in the Gatwick area; it set up displays in local shopping centres, addressed local parish gatherings. And all the time, it stressed that the plans were drafts. Gatwick needed to grow, it said, but how this was to happen was open to discussion; in some cases several options were put before local people.

'I don't think that even protesters enjoy adversarial situations', says Janis Kong.

Local residents just need to know that they can have some input in decisions that affect them. I've found that no one's unreasonable unless they feel they have no control. I've made it my business to meet all the parishes, all the stakeholders. And most people welcome partnership. You're treating them with the dignity they deserve. I now feel I can walk into any village hall anywhere in the vicinity of Gatwick and have a productive meeting.

The face-to-face discussions enabled Janis and other Gatwick managers to get to the root of local concerns. And for the most part they were issues that BAA Gatwick could address effectively without compromising its overall objectives to grow.

At a senior managers' meeting John Egan said there would be no turning back from the consultative approach. 'The company's core business is investment in sustainable development, and to be successful we have to take our stakeholders with us. Gatwick is adopting the right approach. That's the way we do business now.'

During the consultation exercise, Surrey County Council suggested a sustainability audit of Gatwick's draft development proposal. Consultants from Stanger Science and Environment undertook the audit on behalf of a joint working group of BAA Gatwick, local councils and the sustainability charity, Forum for the Future. By drawing Gatwick's development, environment, employment and transport strategies together, the audit gave the company the basis for a comprehensive sustainable development strategy. Furthermore, results showed where the airport was aligning with the local sustainability agenda.

The report concluded that:

- The increase in employment and economic growth associated with an expansion of airport operations has strong positive alignment with local economic sustainability indicators.
- The airport strengthens local social sustainability indicators through its role in the local community, which includes working with schools (education and qualifications indicators) and initiatives such as the BAA Gatwick Airport Youth Games (recreation and leisure indicators).
- The airport supports some environmental sustainability indicators; for example, increased use of public transport, the wider influence of the airport in encouraging improved environmental performance amongst

its suppliers, and improvements to local river quality through advance-
ments in Gatwick's pollution-control infrastructure and increased
efficiencies in waste management, energy and water consumption.

In July 2000, BAA launched its sustainable development strategy for
Gatwick. Unlike the plans for T5, the document was not the first salvo in
a legal war, but a negotiated settlement. There were no unpleasant
surprises. BAA was offering reassurance to Gatwick's neighbours up front:
150 commitments to protect the local community from the impacts of the
development, 40 of them legally binding. They included obligations to:

- Reduce the size of the area most affected by air noise by 50 per cent;
  Gatwick would continue to encourage airlines to operate the quietest
  types of aircraft by imposing higher landing charges on noisier aircraft
  and fining aircraft that exceed noise limits.
- Invest to reduce ground noise on the airport itself, including a ground-
  run pen for aircraft engine testing. The company would also consider
  constructing more noise barriers, such as earth bunds at key points
  around the edge of the airfield.
- Launch a £100 000 a year independent Community Trust Fund for
  community and environmental projects in areas affected by the airport's
  operations. This will also receive the income from fines imposed on
  airlines which breach noise limits.
- Invest more than £10 million in initiatives to cut down growth in
  road traffic, including a £4 million contribution towards FastWay, a
  high-quality local transport system, and £2 million towards road
  improvements.
- Reduce emissions and protect air quality.
- Undertake landscaping initiatives, both on and off the airport.

'We could have given these commitments at a public inquiry', said Janis
Kong. 'But doing it this way, we knew they genuinely addressed what the
community wants. They haven't been imposed; they have arisen from
straight negotiation with stakeholders. The community benefits through the
resolution of issues, and we get to grow.'

The local community welcomed the consultation prior to the development of detailed plans. A West Sussex County Council councillor described
it as:

a new and adventurous approach to the management of large-scale development on the part of an organisation prepared to meet a responsibility, not only to its customers and shareholders, but to the people who may be adversely affected by a huge growth in business.... [BAA Gatwick] are to be congratulated on their initiative and the way in which they have worked closely with ourselves and our fellow councils who represent residents in West and East Sussex and in Surrey to reach a shared objective – growth in air travel at minimal environmental cost and opportunities to improve on present conditions.

The partnership approach produced all sorts of dividends. For instance, there was a problem with the River Mole, a small river crossing Gatwick's north-west zone. It had to be diverted. The company responded positively to the call of local environmentalists to devise a project that would protect and possibly increase the diversity of habitats and species living in and around it. It worked with local people and the Environment Agency and created what is now seen as a textbook way of recreating and enhancing a natural river habitat. The new stretch of river is now full of life, including populations of fish such as gudgeon, dace, chubb and roach (no, this is not the name of a firm of solicitors!) and birds such as kingfishers, sandpipers and moorhens.

The launch of the consultation strategy and the partnership approach gave BAA no cast-iron guarantees that it would get planning approvals, but when the local planning authority, Crawley Borough Council, adopted the Supplementary Planning Guidance (SPG) for Gatwick's plans, the company was given a reasonable expectation. The SPG provided a framework for planning decisions which effectively meant the local authority was likely to approve Gatwick's planning applications, provided it met its commitments.

For BAA, this was vindication of its ground-breaking consultation process – proof that it could come to an agreement with its neighbours without recourse to the adversarial public inquiry process. In February 2001, it signed the legal agreement with the airport's planning authorities, West Sussex County Council and Crawley Borough Council. To ensure that the interests of the whole community continued to be taken into consideration, these councils signed a Memorandum of Understanding with the other local authorities in the area. Gatwick now had a Contract with the Community, literally.

In the summer of 2001, the airport's £1 billion ten-year investment programme was under way, including a new satellite building at the North Terminal featuring a spectacular passenger bridge, spanning the aircraft taxiway. Further developments will include new piers and satellites, more aircraft and stands, and improvements to the North and South Terminals.

With no public inquiry!

In the authors' view this is a classic illustration of the benefits to a business of a stakeholder approach. It won the company a licence to grow its business, it saved time, money and corporate stress, it achieved a business result in harmony with its neighbours, and left almost everybody involved feeling good about the process and its end result.

Growing Stansted

The second big test of BAA's new mission was (and still is) at Stansted, where over-flow from Heathrow and Gatwick and the arrival of low-cost carriers such as Go were generating a phenomenal rate of growth. From three million passengers in 1994, the airport had climbed to 10 million by the end of 1999. BAA was investing £200 million to develop Stansted's facilities up to the 15 million passenger level for which it had outline planning permission. But with this likely to be reached by 2002, the next phase of Stansted's growth was rising rapidly up the company's agenda.

The theoretical capacity of Stansted's single runway was at least 35 million, and with passenger demand in the south-east expected to double by 2015, and Heathrow and Gatwick's runways already filling up, BAA knew the region would be relying on Stansted.

BAA Stansted's Managing Director, John Stent, was responsible for steering the airport through the 15-million barrier. Like Janis Kong, he saw Contract with the Community as the vehicle to achieve growth with the support and trust of local people. An ex-accountant, he admits he was wary of the initiative in the early days.

> At first I thought it was just Des Wilson rhetoric and well-intentioned but we couldn't afford it. I didn't have to be running Stansted long to see that we couldn't afford not to do it.
>
> I found Stansted's local community was generally supportive of the airport, but many – at least half – felt our expansion to 15 million

passengers was enough. They would only give us the permissions we needed to grow beyond this if they were convinced we were on their side when it came to big environmental issues like road traffic, noise, night flights and urbanisation of rural greenbelt land.

Following the Gatwick model, John planned a massive consultation exercise on the airport's expansion. But in the early evening of 22 December 1999, something happened that shook the confidence of Stansted's neighbours in the airport. The following morning, the national press told the story of what might have been:

'A few hundred yards closer and the result would have been too horrific to contemplate,' said the *Daily Mail*. 'Last night two villages were offering thanks for their incredible escape after a jumbo jet loaded with fuel crashed within sight of their homes and exploded in a fireball, flames shooting 600ft into the air.'

The Korean Air 747 plane came down just after takeoff into part of a forest not far from the M11. What was clearly a disaster for the friends and family of the four crew of the cargo jet was fortunately an escape for Stansted's neighbours. But for all their relief, they now felt a new vulnerability.

The accident happened just before BAA's new Chief Executive, Mike Hodgkinson, was due to make his first public appearance at Stansted in that role. He was to address a meeting of local people to announce the consultation process. Knowing that the company would soon be applying for planning permission for a major expansion of the airport, he faced a dilemma. Failing to mention the need for expansion would be disingenuous, a violation of the principles of BAA's new mission statement. Yet discussing expansion, when local people were questioning the safety of current levels of air traffic, was highly insensitive.

'When in doubt, always follow the mission statement', John Egan had always said, and that is what Mike decided to do. Despite the fact that he knew he was facing a worried audience, anxious for reassurance after the crash, he told them openly and honestly what the company hoped to achieve in the future:

Over the past few years we have developed our Contract with the Community and an essential element of that contract is to develop our airports with the trust and support of our neighbours. We know we can only do this if we are open at all times about our needs and

expectations. So I'm going to say to you today that I do not believe
the growth of Stansted will end at 15 million passengers per annum.

Mike acknowledged the local concerns about increased road traffic and
noise, and the threat to the rural character of the area from encroaching
urbanisation. He explained how BAA would continue to minimise demand
for new housing by spreading the airport's employment benefits to areas
requiring economic regeneration like north-east London. And then he
floated the figure of 25 million passengers per year:

> I know that to some of you my proposal today will be of great
> concern. I hope, however, that you will feel able to work with us
> constructively to review the issues as they arise and to help allay
> any unnecessary concerns:

As it had done at Gatwick, BAA wanted to discuss with local people how
it could achieve expansion in a way that was acceptable to them. And
Mike's candour was appreciated. The meeting was surprisingly positive,
and the initial consultations that followed were constructive. John Stent and
his team then embarked on a full-scale consultation programme. An update,
the first of five, was placed in the local press, including a letter from John:

> Before we ask our local planning authority for permission to
> develop our facilities, we want to provide every opportunity to
> take account of your views.... We have identified a number of
> issues which we believe are important. We are appointing
> consultants to investigate the impact of these issues at about 25
> million passengers per annum.

The update set out the consultation process. Having heard back from
local people on the issues set out in the first update, BAA would publish
a formal consultation document, including the results of the consultants'
studies and measures to address local concerns. John Stent and his staff
would then present the detailed findings to the local community in a
series of presentations and a travelling exhibition.

BAA launched this phase of the consultation in October 2000. The
company asked for further feedback and offered local people assurances
that the expansion:

- Would use existing resources more effectively. The passenger terminal would be extended by two bays and development would be kept within the airport boundary.
- Would not require a second runway. The expansion would increase use of the existing runway.
- Would not require additional new housing allocations. Those approved and emerging in council plans would be sufficient to cater for the growth of the airport and the wider area.
- Would not lead to congestion on the local roads. New infrastructure such as the M11 slip roads and A120 improvements would accommodate traffic demand.

In fact road congestion was the issue that concerned people above all else. The company's five-year transport plan already included 34 targets and commitments. But as a result of the consultation process, BAA moved to do more to reassure local residents.

By May 2001, when it launched its Company Travel Plan, the company was proposing a raft of measures to persuade Stansted's staff and passengers to leave their cars at home, including a future investment of £450 million in transport systems serving the airport, £250 million of it by BAA. The Company Travel Plan set out how 1.2 million car journeys would be removed from local roads every year by 2010. Measures include giving BAA staff £110 a year for handing in their car parking pass, charging a public transport levy of 30p on public car parking and £10 on annual staff car park passes, and investing £500000 a year in cycling initiatives and local bus services to help them extend their operating hours and improve their frequency, reliability and quality. For example, the important local Harlow–Sawbridgeworth–Bishops Stortford–Stansted corridor could be served by a bus every 30 minutes, 24 hours a day, seven days a week – a service unheard of in a rural community, benefiting not just passengers for the airport, but people in the wider community.

As a result of the £450 million investment and all these measures, BAA estimated that in 2010, there would be a million fewer vehicles on Stansted's roads than would otherwise be the case.

Even before the Company Travel Plan was launched, BAA had received some encouraging feedback from local residents. In March 2001, six months into the consultation, a MORI opinion poll of 1000 local people, including those in areas most affected by noise, suggested that local people tended to think the airport was 'responsive to the community' and 'open and honest.' Four out of five felt favourable towards it, and two out of three said they supported the proposal for the expansion.

Some misunderstanding in the autumn of 2001 over a plan to create a standby runway facility at the airport tested relationships to the full, but the goodwill reflected by the Mori poll proved once more the value of both the community relations strategy and the kind of open approach Mike Hodgkinson had encouraged. Planning permission for the standby runway was granted by November of that year.

Adopting the Sustainability Agenda

John Egan retired as chief executive in October 1999 and Des Wilson as director of corporate and public affairs in June 2000. By then Contract with the Community was well entrenched but John's successor, Mike Hodgkinson, decided to go a stage further. Convinced by experience that the company's best chance of growing to cater for demand lay in embracing the concerns of its airports' neighbours, he decided to adopt the sustainability agenda and give a lead to the industry. He began his campaign by challenging environmentalists in a speech to an Air Transport Conference in December 2000:

> The problem with the current debate on aviation in the UK is that instead of encouraging a common approach to find workable solutions to issues, the various parties have been encouraged to fight each other from polarised and irreconcilable positions. This is a reflection of our adversarial 'winner takes all' approach to public debate and decision-making. Frankly, I think that we have got this all wrong.
>
> The question that we have been fighting each other over, 'Should the UK have a vibrant and growing aviation industry or protect its environment?' is now widely recognised as the wrong question to have been asking.
>
> What we should have been asking is how the aviation industry can be encouraged to develop sustainably, so that the benefits can be reaped for the environment, for society and for the economy. There are real challenges to face up to, but I believe that sustainable growth

can be achieved if we address the issues openly and constructively, and if the right incentives, structures and resources are put into meeting the challenge.

The environmental challenge is to address the contribution of aviation to climate change, bringing it within the international framework of the Kyoto agreement to reduce greenhouse gas emissions; to take further action on noise, local air quality and surface access; and to deal with issues such as renewable energy, biodiversity and water quality and consumption.

The social challenge is to harness aviation as a positive force for social change and social inclusion. Airports can play vital roles in supporting their local communities and have pioneered new approaches to stakeholder involvement and dialogue. We must build on these strengths.

And the economic challenge is to use aviation as a catalyst for national, regional and local economic regeneration, as well as to provide large numbers of good-quality learning and development opportunities for workers at all levels, including among low-skilled males, where employment opportunities have been declining.

Let's be clear about what is at stake here. It is not only a question of the sustainability of aviation: it is a question of the sustainability of UK plc. Governments abroad are forging ahead with the development of airport infrastructure – usually with public money – harnessing this growing industry's economic and social potential, and reinforcing their country's competitiveness in the global economy.

He outlined what the company had been doing and then challenged all the stakeholders in the debate: 'While BAA can agree to conditions over which we have control, we are only one piece in the jigsaw.' Airports could go a long way in helping to reduce the effects of noise. BAA had built noise walls and installed fixed electrical ground power units to reduce the use of aircraft engines on the ground, and it fined departing aircraft which exceeded noise limits, generating funds for local good causes. With all this, however, there was a limit to what it could do.

Air traffic control (ATC) could also play an increasing part in keeping aircraft on track, and in the effective implementation of continuous descent approach, to reduce the surge from aircraft engines on the landing approach.

And, of course, engine and aircraft manufacturers could play their part by developing and manufacturing quieter aircraft. Airlines, too, must play their part, both by improving operational procedures along with ATC and airports, and by bringing quieter aircraft into service more quickly on the routes serving airports with the highest population densities. That meant not only phasing out the Chapter Two aircraft, but also replacing the noisier Chapter Threes. Planning authorities must play their part too, by refusing applications to build residential estates directly under airport flight paths.

He also, however, challenged the environmental movement:

> It's all too easy to stand on the sidelines attacking the aviation industry, but it's hardly constructive. Instead, engage with us in constructive discussions, not confrontation. Drop the purely ideological opposition and start thinking practically. Help us to achieve common objectives.

He did not duck the fact that people would have to pay more for air travel:

> Let no one doubt that environmentally-sustainable solutions for aviation will inevitably mean paying a bit more for air travel. I recognise that airlines are facing difficult times, but the extra cost per passenger doesn't have to be very large. An extra £1 per passenger on landing charges, for example, would currently generate an additional £170 million a year, and this would increase as passenger numbers grow.

There was a message for government also:

> This certainly isn't simply a question of taxing aviation fuel. If the Government's priority on noise is to encourage airlines to bring in quieter aircraft, then the Government has to make it financially viable for airlines to do this. It should consider fiscal incentives – like it has already done for shipping – which could be offset by the boost in Exchequer revenues from the UK aerospace industries supplying components for these new aircraft.
>
> If the Government wants to reduce emissions, then it should support industry initiatives to do this. BAA is already committed to reducing carbon dioxide emissions from its airport facilities in line

with the Kyoto targets, equivalent to a 60 per cent per passenger reduction on 1990 levels by 2010, and we are committed to obtaining 10 per cent of our electricity from renewable sources by 2010.

But this is not cheap and to go still further will increase our costs even more. As a regulated company, we are prevented from simply putting up our prices to pay for this.

Government must decide the priorities for sustainability. It must use the White Paper to create a framework which provides the right regulatory mechanisms, economic instruments and incentives for sustainable solutions for aviation growth.

We look to Government for decisive leadership and support. On big issues, such as major airport developments.... Government should take the conflict out of the process by taking the big decisions, and then leave the interested parties to agree the appropriate conditions, with time limits, proper case management and, if necessary, professional mediation.

In March 2001 Mike Hodgkinson spoke to the leading forum of the aviation industry, the Aviation Club. Here he was addressing a key group, the airlines, whose impatience for decisions on a third runway for the south-east was being widely broadcast. He reminded his audience that:

The public inquiry into Gatwick's second terminal took 75 days. Terminal 4 took 93 days. Stansted took 175 days and the second runway at Manchester took two years. The Terminal 5 public inquiry took 4 years. In fact assuming no more delays, the whole Terminal 5 process will have taken a staggering 20 years, by the time it opens in 2007. The UK can't afford to wait that long to get new runway capacity. By 2013, Heathrow, with T5, will be full, Gatwick will be full, Stansted will be full, and probably Luton and City as well.

So how would the industry go about getting this capacity?

Well, it can no longer draw up plans in isolation, submit them, and prepare for long public inquiries. Communities are becoming more concerned about their quality of life, less tolerant, better able to voice their concerns, and more effective in their opposition. The only way to break out of this vicious spiral is to address the issues which concern local communities. So that airports can grow with their consent, instead of in the face of their opposition. This isn't just an aspiration – it is what government expects and, what government requires.

This means that aviation has to put sustainability at the core of development, and face up to the environmental and social challenges that growth presents.

The environmental challenge is to address the contribution of aviation to climate change, taking action to reduce greenhouse gas emissions; to take further action on noise, local air quality and surface access; and to deal with issues such as renewable energy.

The social challenge is to harness aviation as a positive force for social change and inclusion. Airports can play vital roles in supporting their local communities, and have pioneered new approaches to stakeholder involvement. We must build on these strengths.

And the economic challenge is to use aviation as a catalyst for national and local economic regeneration, as well as to provide large numbers of good-quality job opportunities.

Our licence to grow depends on how we tackle these issues.

It was to this audience stunning stuff. But it was put in the context of the over-riding concern of everyone present: capacity to grow.

Aviation is a fantastic industry to be in. It has tremendous potential for growth. But I believe that if we are to continue to grow, then an open, co-operative, constructive and partnership approach is the only way forward. The argument is going in our direction. The alternative – which is inconceivable – is for aviation to slip into the near-terminal decline that we are witnessing in the rail industry. We cannot allow that to happen and neither can the government. Because it wouldn't just be the aviation industry that declined – it would be London! Do we really want Paris, Frankfurt and Amsterdam to run off with all the prizes? I think not! But if things are going our way, we must be careful not to overplay our hand. We need to help policy makers to take the difficult decisions which will allow us to grow, and that means making those decisions easier to justify. The constructive, partnership approach to sustainable development, which serves our local interests well, will also serve the national interests, and help us in the aviation industry to secure our future.

This may to the reader seem unexceptional. But there was no way that a BAA chief executive would have spoken like this less than a decade earlier.

It has been a matter of some regret that the environmental movement has not taken up more enthusiastically BAA's challenge to cooperate. But the most respected environmentalists, Jonathon Porritt and Paul Ekins of Forum for the Future, and John Elkington of SustainAbility, have all publicly acknowledged the changes that have taken place and have contributed constructively to them. Porritt spoke to BAA's annual management conference (the first environmentalist ever to do so) and Paul Ekins joined a group advising the company on how to make Terminal 5 a 'green building'. Elkington also advised the company.

Of course the company sometimes slips back. Of course it still has a long way to go. Of course the day when the aviation industry is genuinely sustainable is probably many years away. But the BAA story is the story of a company that listened: to its advisors, to its neighbours, to – if you like – the march of history itself. And it is a company that set about doing things properly, at considerable expense. Its approach has not been a cosmetic one. As a result it has won approval for a major project at Heathrow with broad political and public support, including majority support in the local community, and has won local backing to grow Gatwick without a public inquiry. These are major achievements.

In the next chapter we go into even more detail, not least because we are determined to show this programme is about substance, not rhetoric, so let's summarise its message: it is that BAA's Contract with the Community is a wide-ranging, carefully thought out, expensive, but environmentally and socially worthwhile programme matched by few companies. It is that corporate citizenship is hard work, but immensely rewarding. It is that only by taking the concept into the core of the company and reflecting it in action at every level that you can claim to be at the forefront of change in this area.

CHAPTER 4

BAA's Contract With the Community
What it Is and How it Works

As we have seen, BAA's stakeholders range from those directly involved – airline and passenger customers, employees, business partners and, of course, investors – to those more indirectly involved, national and local government, and local communities. Contract with the Community is the programme that seeks to address the concerns and meet the needs of that second group. In this chapter we seek to show that it is a programme that has real substance.

In the process of developing Contract with the Community the company has moved to align its strategy with national and local government, first in relation to the government's four objectives for sustainable development: effective environmental protection, prudent use of natural resources, social progress, and the maintenance of high and stable levels of economic growth and employment. Because this sets the tenor of regional and local plans, BAA's priorities are therefore also aligned with those of its local authorities so that the company not only speaks the same language as its local stakeholders, but can also contribute positively to their agendas.

As we have already made clear, a problem for BAA is that many of the steps which would enhance the sustainability of its airports are beyond the company's direct control. And BAA stakeholders often have conflicting interests. The best the company can do is to act properly itself and, where it has no direct control, influence its stakeholders. Some of the dilemmas were recognised in an internal strategy document:

- We need to maintain healthy relationships with all our stakeholders and work with them to deliver our objectives. For example, in urging our tenants and business partners to change the way they behave, we must recognise the separate pressures on these businesses to be competitive and profitable.
- We need to continue to influence external organisations to review fiscal and other policies which currently act as barriers to our programme.

- We need to promote our objectives in the context of society's needs and expectations. For instance, we are currently urging airline operators to reduce their waste at the same time as airline users expect high quality packaging for in-flight products. How do we strike the balance?

BAA's strategy for sustainable development embraces three things:

- First, *its policies*: building awareness of, and commitment to sustainable development into its policies in a diverse range of areas, from procurement to landing charges.
- Second, *its processes*: cross-functional boards and committees, some championed by a board director or airport managing director, are supporting the integration of sustainable development into the fibre of the company. Sustainability is included in the core competencies for employees, whose performance is assessed annually. Assessment of senior managers includes a direct link between the sustainable development performance of the company and their bonus scheme.
- Third, *its management systems*: company and airport-level sustainable development programmes are supported by integrated management systems which have long-term objectives and annual targets. Historically they have been focused on environmental and health and safety performance, but the company is looking at ways to extend their scope to address all aspects of its sustainable development programme. BAA also conducts internal audits of the environmental management systems in each of its businesses, in the UK and overseas, using a process consistent with ISO 14001 guidelines.

Let us look at how it all works, beginning with the environment.

Environmental Sustainability

Environmental pressure groups are naturally suspicious when big business adopts the language of sustainability. The only way companies like BAA can truly prove their credentials is by setting quantifiable objectives in partnership with their stakeholders, and achieving them. Thus medium to long-term corporate environmental objectives are established for the company as a whole, while the individual airports produce local environmental objectives and annual targets which are reported in their local sustainability reports and on the BAA Internet site, www.baa.co.uk/sustainabilitity. The sustainability performance of the group as a whole is summarised in the company's annual report and accounts, which are also published on the website. For the last three years, an independent agency has verified BAA's annual report, and its recommendations are incorporated into the company's environmental strategy.

To give leadership to its customers, business partners and suppliers, the company provides incentives through airport charges and contracts with suppliers, and uses environmental considerations in the selection process for new suppliers, service providers and contractors.

With plans to invest £6 billion on new and improved facilities at Heathrow, Gatwick and Stansted over the next 10 years, the company is one of the construction industry's largest clients, and it uses its influence to argue for a sustainable approach to construction across the whole supply chain. In the year 2000, BAA launched an Environmental Construction Awards scheme to encourage environmental best practice, both inside and outside the company. In the year 2000–01, the overall winner was the joint BAA/AMEC Pavement Team, which is responsible for laying 1.3 million square feet of concrete pavement at the airports every year. By recycling concrete, reducing the amount of new concrete used and reducing the cement content of concrete, the team cut the amount of carbon dioxide released as a result of their work by 46 per cent, equivalent to 47 000 tonnes since 1995.

In the year 2000 BAA signalled its intention to produce a step change in its environmental performance with the publication of five medium to long-term objectives (2005–10) in the areas of greatest concern to its local and national stakeholders:

- climate change
- local air quality
- noise
- surface transport
- waste.

The objectives are designed to mitigate the impact of business activities on the environment, and align, where appropriate, with the UK national objectives for sustainable development. They are supported by SMART (specific, measurable, achievable, realistic, timebound) annual targets, which are externally audited and verified. In the year 2000–01, 69 per cent of these targets were fully or substantially achieved. The objectives are championed at the highest level within BAA by an executive director, and they are linked to the annual business planning cycle and mainstream business strategies. BAA has given its managers the flexibility to assess business cases on the basis of whole life costs, which increases the viability of certain desirable projects that will take longer than the standard payback period to produce results; these include energy efficiency, waste recycling and renewable energy projects.

Climate Change

The main impacts of aviation on climate change are associated with fossil fuel consumption related to aircraft fuel consumption, energy used in airport buildings, and surface transport fuel. Under the Kyoto agreement, the UK is committed to reducing its emissions of carbon dioxide and other greenhouse gases to 12.5 per cent below 1990 levels by 2008–12. BAA has set its own medium to long-term targets to contribute towards meeting the Kyoto emissions goal. These include:

- A reduction in absolute carbon dioxide emissions on 1990 levels by March 2010. This is equivalent to a 60 per cent reduction per passenger and a saving of approximately 110 000 tonnes of carbon dioxide on forecast missions by 2010. BAA estimates that achieving this objective will save the company £30 million over 10 years.
- Increased use of renewable electricity to 5 per cent by 2003 and 10 per cent by 2010.
- A 20 per cent improvement on current best practice for the energy efficiency of new buildings by efficient energy management and retrofitting of new technology into its existing buildings.
- The development of at least one high-profile demonstration project of integrated photovoltaics within the design of a new building.

Between 1996–97 and 2000–01, emissions of carbon dioxide per passenger fell from 5.47 to 3.5 kg. And despite absolute increases in passenger numbers, total carbon dioxide emissions from the energy used to run the company's seven UK airports fell from 535 743 tonnes to 437 022 tonnes.

In the first full year (2000–01) the company's progress towards its ten-year objective was promising. Most individual airports had achieved emissions impacts below the annual milestone targets which had been set internally. Overall, as an airports group, performance was 3.7 per cent better than the annual milestone target, though total emissions from its seven UK airports rose slightly over the previous year. BAA's CFC refrigerant holdings for refrigeration plant and chilled water systems fell substantially between 1996–97 and 2000–01, from 42.57 tonnes to 9 tonnes.

A utilities review conducted in 2000–01 highlighted a number of initiatives that would be needed to achieve BAA's ten-year objective. These included metering and conservation initiatives to reduce energy consumption by 10 per cent within ten years, exploring the possible role of combined heat and power plants (CHPs), local solar energy schemes, customer/business partner conservation projects and incentives to help them reduce their consumption by 5 per cent, and creating an energy-focused culture in the company by continuous training and communication initiatives.

In addition, BAA is procuring more 'green tariff' electricity and investigating partnerships to expand the supply of renewable energy. A scenario planning exercise on the risks and benefits of investing in an offshore wind-farm development has also been completed, and the business case is being explored with wind facility developers.

Intergovernmental Panel on Climate Change

As a global industry that operates across national boundaries, international air traffic was not covered directly by the Kyoto protocol (assigning emissions to individual nations proved too complex). Instead, countries are pursuing measures to limit or reduce emissions of greenhouse gases through the UN International Civil Aviation Organisation (ICAO). As a first step, ICAO commissioned the Intergovernmental Panel on Climate Change (IPCC) to set up a special working group on aviation and the global atmosphere. This concluded that though there is significant uncertainty over the future contribution of aviation to global warming due to carbon dioxide, the figure is most likely to be 5.6 per cent by 2050, an increase of 2.1 per cent on the current contribution of 3.5 per cent.

Although 3.5 per cent is a relatively small contribution to global warming, BAA recognised that climate change would become a significant issue for the aviation industry, particularly in the light of the forecast growth in aviation and the reliance of aircraft on fossil fuels.

As we have already noted, Mike Hodgkinson has been actively working within the aviation industry, both nationally and internationally, to raise the issue and promote debate into what else can be done.

In spring 2001 the company involved both internal and external stakeholders in a scenario planning exercise on aircraft emissions and climate change, looking specifically at how this issue could affect airports and development over the next 30 years.

The company is currently engaging with the government to support the development of UK political leadership on measures to reduce and/or mitigate aviation's contribution to climate change, producing a sustainable-development forum to promote a sector-wide approach to climate change through dialogue with key stakeholders, and seeking with its regulator to develop mechanisms that encourage its business partners to take up new technologies in order to improve the aviation industry's environmental performance.

Local Air Quality

To reduce airport-generated pollution the company has initiated a wide range of programmes tackling all sources of emissions at its airports, including aircraft, vehicle fleets and other road traffic.

Both Heathrow and Gatwick now have local air quality management strategies. Air quality has been continuously monitored at these airports for the last eight years by AEA Technology, which measures the main air pollutants covered by the UK National Air Quality Strategy. During 2000–01 levels of all pollutants measured at these sites were within limits set by the UK government, with the exception of annual average nitrogen dioxide levels which failed the relevant guideline (this standard is currently exceeded in many urban areas of the UK). Heathrow and Gatwick are working with their local authorities to address air quality management issues. Otherwise, measurements were compliant with current UK-AQS objectives for nitrogen dioxide (hourly average) and PM10 (that is, small particles: 24 hour average).

BAA is also carrying out a programme to reduce aircraft emissions at ground level by installing fixed ground power units to reduce the time aircraft keep their engines running while they are parked on stands, improving ground manoeuvring procedures and the layout of aprons and taxiways to reduce the time between pushback from stand and take-off.

A trial at Heathrow incorporating these factors produced fuel savings of between 3000 and 5000 tonnes: a 3–4 per cent cut in emissions. Heathrow now has fixed electrical ground power installed on 90 per cent of its aircraft stands. It is also the first major UK airport to begin operational trials of pre-conditioned air (PCA). This is used to control cabin temperatures, humidity and ventilation while aircraft are parked on stands. By reducing the need to run auxiliary power units, it will improve local air quality, reduce ground noise and halve the carbon dioxide emissions produced by aircraft on stand. Using PCA with a fixed supply of power from the stand also reduces nitrous oxides and hydrocarbon emissions, which affect local air quality. Up to 0.2 tonnes of carbon dioxide emissions will be saved per hour on a typical Boeing 747 aircraft turnaround.

BAA employs extensive measures to reduce emissions from airside road vehicles; these include placing maximum age limits on airside vehicles and encouraging the use of alternative fuels, providing a 50 per cent rebate to taxis at Heathrow running on low emission alternative fuels, and reducing apron spillage during re-fuelling.

Noise Management

Technological advances have significantly reduced the noise produced by aircraft over the years. Today's aircraft are 20 decibels quieter than aircraft of 30 years ago. And these advances have been paralleled by new operational procedures and noise mitigation measures, which have contributed to a significant reduction in the area and numbers of people annoyed by aircraft noise.

The area considered by the government to be subject to nuisance from aircraft noise has fallen by 73 per cent around Heathrow since 1980, and by 77 per cent around Gatwick. At Gatwick less than 1 per cent of aircraft were off track thanks to the procedures developed in partnership with the airlines and air traffic control.

BAA's central position among all the parties involved – local authorities, local residents' groups, airlines and air traffic controllers, as well as government – enables it to promote a common noise-reduction agenda and to resolve conflicts that arise, particularly between the interests of airlines (and passengers) and local residents. This stewardship role and a range of direct powers give the company significant influence over the noise climate around its airports.

BAA's objective is a reduction in overall noise per passenger of 10 per cent within the area of the 1998 57 Leq contour by 2005, and year-on-year reductions in infringements of noise limits.

Take-offs are routed around densely populated areas on Noise Preferential Routes (NPR) published by the government. These aircraft must stay 'on track', within a 3 kilometre wide corridor. In the year 1999–2000, only 6 per cent of Heathrow aircraft were off-track.

There are also special rules for the use of Heathrow's runways. Most of the time, the airport uses one of its runways for take-offs and the other for landings; switching the landing runway at 3 pm gives the densely populated areas to the east of the airport predictable periods of relief from the noise of landing aircraft.

During the night period (11.30 pm to 6 am) there is a ceiling on the number of flights allowed at all BAA's south-east airports throughout the year and at Glasgow in the summer. The noisiest aircraft cannot be scheduled at any BAA airport. In addition, each south-east airport is allocated a quota of noise between 11.30 pm and 6 am. Noisier aircraft use up more points, so airlines have an incentive to schedule their quietest models. BAA has voluntarily banned some of the noisiest aircraft permitted under the government scheme at Heathrow during this period.

The company also promotes best practice operational procedures to airlines and National Air Traffic Services. For example, in the year 2000 up to 85 per cent of aircraft used the continuous descent approach at Heathrow during the sensitive night-time period. Other techniques which are being assessed include short final approaches, steeper descent angles and curved descents avoiding populated areas.

The company fines airlines that break noise limits. If aircraft exceed government departure-noise limits, the operator is fined and the money is channelled into environmental projects. Over 3 dBA above noise limit, airlines are fined a maximum of £1000; under 3 dBA above noise limit, the fine is a maximum of £500. In addition, airport charges are higher for noisy aircraft: for instance, a 90 per cent differential charge is imposed on noisier Chapter 2 aircraft such as the B747, while there is a 10 per cent discount for the quietest Chapter 3 aircraft, such as the B757.

In sensitive areas closest to local housing, BAA has built earth barriers to block out noise and laid porous asphalt on the roads to reduce tyre disturbance. At Gatwick, the company has also erected a noise wall, certain taxiways have been modified to reduce noise and, aided by a planning condition, the company requires aircraft to be towed to their stand during the night period.

BAA is running a £10 million five-year voluntary noise insulation scheme for the houses around Heathrow within the 69 dBA contour. A total of 3270 houses have been insulated since April 1996. It also operates a walk-in Noise Information Centre at Heathrow, and a 24-hour noise information line for local residents at all its airports.

Surface Transport

Encouraging airport staff and passengers to switch from cars to public transport more often is one of the cornerstones of BAA's sustainable development strategy. The company's UK airports, particularly those in the south-east, remain at the forefront of European performance in this regard. At Heathrow, Gatwick, Stansted and Southampton the average percentage of non-connecting passengers using public transport has risen from 33 per cent in 1996–97 to 34.3 per cent in 2000–01, among the highest in Europe. In Scotland, the figure for 2000–01 is 10.7 per cent, up from 7.3 per cent.

BAA's contribution to integrated transport strategies has made it a reference organisation in the development and management of integrated transport. In February 2001, for example, Heathrow's integrated transport strategy won the airport the first AA award for transport innovation.

BAA's overall integrated transport strategy involves:

- Investment in public transport: BAA has committed £620 million at Heathrow alone and the company has been a catalyst for encouraging investment by others.
- Partnership: BAA has formed partnerships with transport operators, local authorities and other interested parties to provide effective transport solutions for its airports and the surrounding areas.
- Integrated transport plans for airports.

Investment in public transport is one of the government's 13 headline indicators for sustainable development in the UK. BAA's south-east airports are proving that they can act as catalysts, encouraging others to invest in public transport in the south-east region as a whole.

The Heathrow Express has become a symbol of the opportunities that can emerge from a single, albeit very large, public transport investment. Back in the 1980s the company had regarded rail transport as a matter for the rail industry, and while it regretted there was inadequate rail access to Heathrow it could not see what it could do about it. But when the Thatcher government refused to authorise the public sector British Rail to invest, BAA took the momentous decision to do so itself. Work began on the £450 million Heathrow Express in 1994, and over the next four years over 12 000 people and 130 contractors contributed to a project which would become an example of best practice in construction management. In 1997, the partnership approach adopted by the BAA/Balfour Beatty single construction team, following a disastrous tunnel collapse, won the company the Institute of Personnel and Development 'People Management' Award.

The Heathrow Express construction project was also environmentally sensitive. Five miles of the 17-mile route were constructed in tunnels; 18 000 trees were planted; a 2-metre high, 1-metre thick 'green wall' was built to shield houses from the track at Hayes to the north of the airport; three tunnel ventilation fans on farmland were disguised as barns; a wildlife haven was created adjacent to the mainline track (including two new ponds); miniature access shafts were created for field mice, voles, shrews and hedgehogs in railway embankments; and a new lakeside habitat was created for a family of kingfishers.

As the construction project progressed, BAA began to appreciate the strategic opportunities its investment was creating for the development of rail at Heathrow. It undertook a series of feasibility studies which identified possibilities for additional services to the north, south, east and west of the airport.

The opportunities for the Heathrow Express itself were also coming into clearer focus. If it was going to attract Heathrow's passengers out of their cars, BAA knew the service could be no ordinary airport shuttle. It would have to redefine public transport, drawing more from aviation than the traditional rail industry, with sophisticated rolling stock, staff to rival the best in the service sector and full baggage check-in at Paddington.

The strategy worked. Soon after the June launch it was clear that the speed, frequency and quality of the Heathrow Express were attracting people who would never have considered using public transport before. By the end of 1998, its first year, 98 per cent of Heathrow Express passengers said they would use it again and recommend it to their friends. And the service's successful debut was recognised when Heathrow Express was voted 'train operator of the year' by the professional rail industry. Between the launch and the end of the 2000–01 financial year, passenger levels doubled from 50 000 to 100 000 a week: 5 million a year, a third of airport users travelling to and from Central London. As a result, the roads to Heathrow have to cope with 3000 fewer vehicles every day than would otherwise be the case.

The environmental benefits of Heathrow Express extend into London with two green travel initiatives for passengers arriving at Paddington: the Hotel Express, a coach service to a number of central London hotels, and taxi-sharing – a cooperative effort between Heathrow Express, Railtrack and the Licensed Taxi Association in which taxi marshals invite passengers with similar destinations who are willing to share, to jump the queue. They pay a flat rate, which is generally lower than that for single occupancy journey.

Having created the rail infrastructure at Heathrow, and with the Heathrow Express Paddington service using less than half the initial (ten trains an hour) capacity of the tracks and tunnels, BAA turned its attention to filling the spare capacity.

The company's first move was to announce two shuttle services an hour between the airport and Hayes station, 2.5 miles north-east of the airport. Passengers from destinations to the west, including Cardiff, Swindon and Oxford, will connect with the shuttle for the short journey into the airport.

At the time of writing BAA's rail plans were at the mercy of Railtrack's ability to deliver its contribution to an ambitious scenario, but the hope has been that the shuttle is the first stage of a full sister service to the Heathrow Express–Paddington route which BAA hopes to eventually be able to run into St Pancras. The 35-minute service will initially run twice an hour each way, stopping at West Hampstead or Cricklewood, Ealing Broadway and Hayes and Harlington stations. With a catchment area of the City and the eastern side of London's West End, the St Pancras service could be expected to attract 2.8 million passengers in its first year, rising to 4 million with an increase in frequency to four times an hour.

In the longer-term, completion of the Thameslink 2000 project and the second stage of the Channel Tunnel rail link will make St Pancras a major hub with international, national, regional and London Underground connections. This new infrastructure would also create opportunities to extend the St Pancras–Heathrow Express service into the City.

Connecting the track with the South-West mainline at Staines would give destinations to the south and west of Heathrow direct access to the airport for the first time. A detailed feasibility study involving BAA, Railtrack, British

Airways, a number of local authorities and other interested parties has confirmed the feasibility of the £60 million 'Airtrack' project, a network of services into the airport from destinations such as Reading, Guildford, Woking, Clapham Junction and Waterloo or Victoria.

In addition to Airtrack, domestic long-distance services to the Midlands and the North of England could run from Heathrow. And should the Cross-Rail project go ahead, there would be scope for services direct to Heathrow from the City.

As we say, however, these and other ideas were at the time of writing awaiting the recovery of the rail industry from the Hatfield disaster and other problems, and in particular the fate of Railtrack.

The involvement of other organisations prepared to invest in rail services to Heathrow testifies to the powerful catalytic effect of BAA's initial investment. The Heathrow Express story does not end at Heathrow, however. In February 2000, BAA and National Express formed the Airport Express alliance, a partnership to bring together the airport express rail services in the south-east in such a way as to attract more passengers and increase rail's mode share at the three main south-east airports. The first phase is a sales and marketing alliance between Heathrow Express and National Express's Gatwick and Stansted Express services. The alliance brings together the sales and marketing activities of all three operations to create a single point of contact. The second phase of the alliance is a proposal for a new fleet of longer Stansted Express trains and infrastructure enhancements.

Partnerships are now seen as crucial to the development of effective transport solutions. They bring together local authority expertise in planning, economic regeneration and the environment, alongside the private sector's customer focus and skills in marketing analysis. BAA recognised this need in 1995 when it formed the UK's first transport forum at Heathrow. Comprising local and transport authorities, key local businesses and transport operators from the area, it was conceived as both a strategic forum and, through its working groups, a focus for practical problem solving.

Since the creation of the Heathrow Area Transport Forum, the concept has been incorporated into government policy as a model for airports across the country. BAA has launched similar schemes at Gatwick (April 1998) and Stansted (March 1999), and at its Scottish airports in 1999 and 2000.

The bus and coach lane on the M4 spur at Heathrow is an example of the real benefits which airport transport forums can deliver. BAA invested £1.8 million in the scheme, working with the Highways Agency and other parties through the framework of the Heathrow Area Transport Forum. The scheme cut the average peak-hour journey by 9.7 minutes and journey times over a 4-hour period by 3.5 minutes.

In line with the recommendations of the government's White Paper on integrated transport, BAA's airports have formalised their public transport and other initiatives within the framework of Airport Travel Plans. Each airport has now produced its own transport strategy, which includes a series of targets and commitments to increase the number of passengers and staff using public transport.

Airport Transport Plans draw BAA's staff-focused Company Travel Plans into the broader context of transport strategy. BAA's Airport Transport Plans then feed into local and regional plans developed by local authorities in consultation with airport area transport forums. This approach has also made a difference at the other south-east airports.

With hundreds of connections per day, Gatwick's rail links are unrivalled by any UK airport and among the best of any airport in the world. This high frequency creates significant opportunities to attract more airport passengers onto rail. BAA is working with Railtrack and the train operating companies on a range of measures to improve the rail product at the airport. These include developing Gatwick's rail station into a world-class interchange point, improving the range and quality of rail services, and better-targeted marketing campaigns. Over £100 million is being invested in new-generation rolling stock for the Gatwick Express, the 30-minute non-stop service, which runs every 15 minutes from London's Victoria. The fleet is now the most modern in the UK.

Stansted's rail services also hold significant potential for the future. The airport's integral railway station is connected to the main line to London and Cambridge, and stopping services already run to the airport from the Midlands and the North, as well as London's Liverpool Street Station. As Stansted expands, the 42-minute Stansted Express service from Liverpool Street offers the greatest potential for increasing the percentage of airport passengers travelling by rail. In the short term, the service is being improved with on-board catering facilities and the company is anxious to extend its 15-minute frequency throughout the day during the week. In the longer term, BAA and National Express, its partner in Airport Express, are proposing that the service be separated from the remainder of the West Anglia Great Northern franchise and awarded as a 20-year franchise to the Airport Express joint venture.

The franchise proposal to be put forward by BAA/National Express will include the provision of a new fleet of longer trains (similar to the high-quality Heathrow Express fleet) and an infrastructure improvement, which would triple the capacity of the Stansted service. In the longer term, as Stansted's passenger numbers grow, there is potential to operate an additional Airport Express London service to St Pancras. This could either operate through London, using the capacity created by the Thameslink 2000 project, or to the St Pancras mainline station with connections to Gatwick and Heathrow airports, the Channel Tunnel and many UK regions.

Strong bus and coach networks are central to BAA's vision for its airports as leading inter-modal hubs. Heathrow is already Britain's busiest bus and coach hub, with over 1600 services per day to 1000 local and national destinations. 10 per cent of Gatwick's passengers arrive and depart on 320 local bus services and 440 express coach services per day. At Stansted also, bus and coach operators have adapted quickly to the airport's fast growth and the changing patterns of demand. As well as the £1.8 million bus and coach lane on the M4 spur, Heathrow has invested £3 million in the Central Terminal Area bus and coach station, including airport-style information monitors at each bus and coach stop. The company has also formed marketing partnerships with Express coach operators to promote their services to airport passengers.

This is partly financed by passengers. Heathrow was the first airport to introduce a levy on car parking to contribute towards transport initiatives. Contributions of 25p and £12 are taken from public car parking fees and annual staff car park season tickets respectively, generating £1.9 million every year for the airport's Transport Fund. BAA invests a further £500 000 in schemes to improve transport at the airport. The scheme is now operating at all BAA's south-east airports.

The government's White Paper on the future of transport called on employers to develop company travel plans to encourage staff to leave their cars at home for journeys to and from work. BAA's range of practical and progressive measures has become a model for other airports and centres of high employment throughout the country. This success is despite the obvious challenges associated with airports, such as shift patterns (typically around 40 per cent of staff report to work before 8 am) and the fact that BAA staff account for less than 10 per cent of the work forces at its airports.

Since 1995, the company has helped to fund improvements to 20 services, including higher frequencies, greater reliability, improved quality and targeted marketing. While bus patronage decreased by 25 per cent nationally, passengers on Heathrow services increased by 100 per cent between 1995 and 1997. On some routes the growth rate has been greater; for example, after the 285 service was supported by British Airways and BAA, patronage increased by 120 per cent.

Most local bus services around Heathrow have been made free to all users. Funded jointly with British Airways at a cost of £300 000 per year, the scheme is designed to attract staff who would not normally use public transport. A similar initiative has been introduced at Gatwick. This airport is contributing £4 million to the £27 million FastWay project to introduce a network of twenty-first century superbuses to the Horley/Crawley area, a centre for many airport staff. The high quality service will incorporate features such as dedicated bus lanes, priority at traffic lights, and sections of guided track away from other road users. Twelve buses will pass through Gatwick every hour in each direction, and the service will operate extended hours, seven days a week. Gatwick workers living south of Crawley will have their journey time cut from 45 to 20 minutes as a result of the scheme. Gatwick has set itself a target of doubling the percentage of its staff from the area choosing to use public transport within three years of FastWay's successful implementation. Until then the company is investing £1 million in 'Airport Direct' a conventional quality bus service, which serves FastWay core routes. The service has extended hours of operation suited to Gatwick's shift patterns.

BAA was the first private sector company in the UK to launch an integrated public transport travelcard. The Airports Travelcard – the first of its kind in Europe – gives users up to 80 per cent discount on the regular season ticket price for commuting to and between BAA's three south-east airports on most services. Staff travelcards have also been introduced at Glasgow, giving unlimited use of all airport and many network services.

Although Gatwick is served by 930 rail services a day, only 5 per cent of BAA airport staff use rail to commute to work. Following a survey that identified cost as one of the main reasons, BAA Gatwick negotiated a Traincard discount scheme, which offers up to 60 per cent off season tickets. BAA aims to increase the number of its staff at Gatwick using rail by 10 per cent by 2008.

A major deterrent to using public transport is often the need to change trains or buses, so improving the quality of interchanges and connections is central to the company's travel plans. For example, the Hatton Cross London

Underground and bus station at the south-east entrance to Heathrow acts as a major interchange point for employees at the airport and in the surrounding area. Six per cent of the airport's 68 000 staff use the tube, making it the single most important mode for commuting, particularly for employees living in west London and the local Borough of Hounslow. With BAA support, bus services to the station were increased by 90 per cent and the station approaches were re-engineered to make bus and pedestrian access easier.

The company has developed the Heathrow Travel Net to enable airport staff to access information on public transport routes and travel options to and from the airport, via a desktop PC system and common PCs for staff in non-desk jobs. The service is thought to be the UK's first for planning journeys on different modes and across boundaries. It includes national timetables for Railtrack and National Express coaches, together with local services over a 50-mile radius.

BAA is also making walking and cycling to work at its airports easier. At Gatwick, it has developed an on-airport cycle track in partnership with SUSTRANS, the Cyclists' Touring Club and local authorities. Other improvements, mirrored elsewhere in the Group, are free use of airport showers, lockable cycle racks with storage, discounts on cycle purchase, clothing and safety training and free twice-yearly check-ups by a 'bike doctor'. Glasgow has also opened a new cycle track. At Heathrow, BAA is establishing a network of cycle routes and Greenways in conjunction with the Highways Agency and the local boroughs. By 2002, the company is committed to doubling the number of airport employees cycling to work. The Greenways offer the wider community around Heathrow efficient and attractive cycle routes away from heavy traffic, between home, work and major attractions and facilities. When completed the network will link 9 miles of existing cycle and pedestrian routes, 45 miles of previously proposed routes, and 6 miles of newly proposed routes.

Finally, Heathrow, Gatwick, Stansted and Glasgow operate formal car-sharing schemes based on the principles of computer dating to match potential partners. Benefits include priority parking and discounted fuel.

Waste Management

Waste management activity is focused on procurement, terminal management, retail and property. In the year 2000, the company appointed a group

Waste Manager, who is responsible for overseeing contracts with waste disposal companies, for waste measurement and sharing good practice within BAA.

All the company's business units – from terminals to new developments – are now required to have a sustainable waste-management plan. The plans include baseline measures, specific waste targets, indicators, a reporting process, mitigation measures such as recycling and energy recovery, and a programme to incentivise suppliers to reduce waste.

Corporate Citizenship and the Three Es

BAA's corporate citizenship is based on open and honest dialogue with its neighbours and positive involvement in the affairs of the community.

As well as an ongoing discussion about its plans and activities with the local authorities, BAA has for many years had its own consultative committees for each airport. Established as part of the privatisation process, they are independently chaired and draw their membership from a wide range of local representatives, including environmental groups and local businesses, as well as local councillors from 36 local authorities representing over 10 million people. The committees help to keep local residents involved in and informed of airport plans, and provide an umbrella for working groups dealing with particular issues such as noise. Reports and debate with these committees, when added to the individual airport reports available to all the community, ensure an open approach and accountability to local opinion.

The other key element of corporate citizenship is to seek to make a creative and positive contribution to the community. This is not about trying to buy popularity; the company knows that does not work. It is about balancing the negative impacts with a positive one so that it can hold up its head as a citizen of the area. The company and its employees invest both money and voluntary time into this. The financial donations include injecting around £1 million a year into local causes, half from its own charity, the BAA Twenty-First Century Communities Trust, and the remainder from funds raised through noise fines and other airport sources such as foreign-coin collection boxes.

By giving their time and expertise to community-based activities, employees acting voluntarily add value in a way that cash alone can never do. The company encourages them by paying for them to spend up to six days per year on community projects, and by linking external community activities with the personal development of staff by encouraging them to undertake community initiatives to meet specific personal learning and growth objectives. Personal contributions of staff are recognised through 'good neighbour awards' at its annual airport staff conferences.

BAA helps young burns survivors, so ten members of the Heathrow Fire Service climbed the three highest peaks in Scotland, England and Wales – Ben Nevis, Scafell Pike, and Snowdon – to raise money for the Burned Children's Fund. Another ten members of Heathrow's property team helped to create a conservation area at a Farnham Common infants' school, and 20 members of the airport's public affairs team helped a local school to transform some wasteland into a nature trail. Staff from the two main Scottish airports cycled the towpath of the Forth and Clyde canal to raise money for children's hospices. A Gatwick property team learned sign language to help a school for the deaf. A Southampton personnel officer mentored a difficult local teenager who constantly played truant; the girl's prospects were transformed, she returned to school, passed exams and went to college. A Terminal 2 security guard organised parties and trips for local kids with special needs; another security guard walked from one end of the country to another to raise money for a special needs school. Volunteers from Southampton Airport helped build a square-rigger for the Jubilee Sailing Trust. And we could list many others.

The priorities of BAA's Community Support Programme are the three Es: Environment, Education and Employment. Let us consider each in turn.

Environment

The company contributes to the greening of the surrounding areas. Heathrow is supporting an ambitious £2.7 million five-year scheme to breath new life into the A4/M4 corridor with tree-lined boulevards, hedgerow, woodland, and parkland. In a similar initiative for the west London rail corridor, BAA's Heathrow Express operating company is working with other rail companies and London boroughs such as Ealing. Heathrow and Stansted airports are supporting the Trees for London project and another campaign in Essex.

Heathrow also sponsors 'Bulbs Around the World', an annual Groundwork Thames Valley initiative which supplies 110 000 daffodil and crocus bulbs to 270 community groups and schools, and donated £60 000 to turn a landfill site in Slough into a new public park with landscaping, tree planting, lighting and a school ecology study area. Heathrow also funds £ 30 000 of Environment Awards for local school and community sustainable-development projects. The applications are judged according to how well they meet local Agenda 21 themes, such as whether the project involves the community in all stages, whether there will be lasting benefits and whether its use of materials supports the local economy.

Gatwick supports the Horley-Crawley Countryside Management Project, which undertakes woodland management, hedge restoration, pond clearance, and meadow management projects in the countryside surrounding the airport. The company sponsors the project's Land Rover, and airport staff regularly help with coppicing local woods, litter clearing and planting schemes.

Education

Education is the second of the three Es which underpin the company's community contributions. BAA is working with the London Leadership Centre to develop leadership skills among the capital's head teachers. The two organisations have collaborated on a number of training initiatives, including a seminar for head teachers and school governors on performance management in schools. It has become a member of the national steering group of 'Partners in Leadership', a joint Business in the Community and Teacher Training Agency initiative to improve the ability of principals to make hard decisions about staffing, budgets and pupil behaviour. As part of the initiative, a number of company managers have become mentors to local head teachers. John Egan personally took part in this scheme.

Another initiative has been to link managers with local schools (50 managers participated in the case of Gatwick, 12 as business governors). They involve themselves in school life, drawing on their business skills and experience to advise teachers and identify opportunities for BAA support. BAA airports have hosted a large number of teacher workshops on specialist subjects such as the use of IT.

Heathrow runs a programme of work-related learning days at the airport, including workshops on customer service, and a 'design an airport terminal' challenge for Year 9 students. Heathrow staff have also given lectures on customer service to GNVQ students in South Bucks and Hillingdon. The schemes help students to improve their understanding of airport issues and develop the skills needed for working in industry. All BAA airports organise work experience for local students, but many also take part in more formal structured programmes. Gatwick and Scottish Airports, for example, participate in the Young Enterprise Scheme, which is designed to develop the business acumen of local sixth formers. The students develop an idea for a product or service within the formal structure of their own company and BAA staff act as mentors.

Glasgow airport also participates in 'Project Q', which is part of the Quality Scotland Initiative. In the first half of 2001, groups of senior pupils from local secondary schools surveyed Glasgow Airport staff awareness of environmental issues and local community activity. They developed communication packages to address the gaps and their leaflet on how to get involved in the local community is now part of the induction process for new staff at the airport.

With a £300 000 five-year sponsorship, BAA is one of the main business supporters of the Young Engineers' Clubs in England, Wales and Scotland. The scheme is designed to promote the importance of engineering to young people by giving them practical experience. In addition to the financial support from BAA, many of the company's professional engineering staff assist their local young engineers' clubs with practical engineering challenges. Airport-related projects have included a runway lighting problem and the design of a baggage handling system. Gatwick set a similar challenge for Year 10 pupils from six local schools across West Sussex. Working alongside BAA staff they designed a check-in desk for a fictitious new airline targeting the youth market.

Gatwick airport has supported eight local schools in their bids for 'specialist status', a Department for Education initiative to create centres of excellence in the disciplines needed for the workforce of the future. Accreditation, which brings significant extra resource into the schools, requires the Gatwick-area schools to match funding provided by the government with private sponsorship – £10 000 from BAA. The airport-supported schools are split equally between language and technology specialist status.

Gatwick has developed partnerships with two education action zones, Brighton and Hove and New Addington (London Borough of Croydon). Education action zones are a government initiative to raise standards of literacy and numeracy in areas with high levels of social deprivation and low academic achievement.

BAA produces a wide range of curriculum-based teaching resources for key stages one, two and three, GCSE geography and Scottish environmental studies 5–14. For example, the company has invested £60 000 in the primary literacy pack, 'Jumbo and Jet', which it has developed with education consultants and Surrey County Council. The high quality pack contains a book, teachers' guide and work sheets and tells the story of a journey through Heathrow from the perspective of two cartoon characters. Staff from BAA's corporate office in London Victoria help to teach reading in local schools as part of the national literacy programme.

Following the success of the BAA Millennium Youth Games, the company's airports remain title sponsors of their local youth games. The London Heathrow Youth Games, for example, is one of the largest sporting events in the world in terms of participant numbers. In 2000, BAA Heathrow made a contribution of £130 000 to the event, which attracted 20 000 participants – more than the Sydney Olympics. Competitors represented all 33 London boroughs in 50 sports.

Employment

The third of the three Es is employment. The company is working with local authorities to regenerate economic black spots through a range of measures: west and east London are being supported by their local airports, Heathrow and Stansted, while Gatwick is focusing increasingly on the deprived areas on the south coast. The main vehicles for this are projects supported by the government's Single Regeneration Budget, to which BAA contributes additional funds. Heathrow supports three major Single Regeneration Budget (SRB) initiatives in London: the Hayes and West Drayton Partnership (which John Egan chaired for a time), the Feltham First Regeneration Programme and the Southall Regeneration Partnership. Gatwick supports an SRB project in Brighton and Hove, and contributes to the area's education action zone.

In addition to significant cash contributions to projects within these areas, the company contributes senior management time and expertise. For example BAA's chief executive, Mike Hodgkinson, is Chair of the Hayes and West Drayton Partnership, and Heathrow's managing director, Roger Cato, sits on the SRB board. BAA Gatwick is represented on the steering group of the Brighton and Hove SRB.

Airports are a constant source of new jobs, but local people do not always have the appropriate skills to take advantage of this. BAA is tackling the issue through 'New Deal', the government scheme to get the long-term unemployed back into work. Through subsidised work placements at its airports, the company is helping to develop skills and confidence. A prime example is the Construction Training Centre at Heathrow, where BAA and its partners in the Airport Construction Alliance are training New Deal local residents to take advantage of the thousands of construction jobs that arise at the airport every year.

The fast expansion of Stansted is creating another mismatch between jobs and people. In this case the sheer volume of the new jobs cannot be accommodated by the local labour market alone. The airport currently employs 9500 people and it is estimated that this will increase to around 16 000 if the airport wins planning approval to handle around 25 million passengers a year.

BAA has launched a major recruitment campaign to attract employees from east and north east London, where the populations are larger and unemployment levels are relatively high. The programme includes road shows in which airport companies demonstrate the wide range of airport jobs available in retailing, security, airlines, catering and aircraft maintenance. Skills training is also available for hospitality jobs at the airport. The London Borough of Haringey is considering an airport-specific training programme which would lead to a national qualification. For the first six months of the scheme, participants have their transport expenses paid by the Employment Service, and after this period they still qualify for subsidised travel with the Airports Travel Card. Recruits from the Tottenham Hale area have access to the Stansted Express, which stops at the local station.

In a similar initiative, Gatwick has introduced bus services to attract airport workers from unemployment black spots on the south coast. As the airport expands to accommodate 40 million passengers a year by 2008, it is estimated that 4000 more jobs will be created. Gatwick is working with Sussex Enterprise and airlines to promote job opportunities through the airport, a unique, self-funded, website-based partnership.

BAA has also invested over £ 200 000 in Foyer projects around its airports. These locally-based centres provide low-cost accommodation, life-skills development and employment training opportunities within a safe and supportive environment for young people who lack parental support.

As part of its policy to ensure that its airport communities share directly in the wealth generated by its airports, BAA has a number of initiatives to assist local companies in winning business from the airports. The 'Heathrow Area Business Opportunities' programme, for example, helps local companies to understand and equip themselves for business opportunities at the airport. The initiative includes a 'Meet the Buyers' event at Heathrow, organised in partnership with the six local authorities, Business Link London West and SHAPE.

The three Es programme is a carefully considered one, aimed at the key concerns of the communities around the company's airports. As we noted earlier, the programme is based on the simple proposition that if the airport brings some discomfort in terms of noise and traffic along with its many economic benefits, it can balance that discomfort further by contributing to the well-being of the community and, in particular, its most vulnerable members. Too easily dismissed by sceptics as a goodwill gesture, it is a quietly operated, extensive and long-term programme intended to make a real difference to people's lives. And it does.

Acting Differently

In every way the company is trying to act differently. For instance, it scored another 'win–win' with its approach to archaeology on the site for Terminal 5. Developers have traditionally treated excavation as a pain in the neck, to be ignored for as long as possible, then acted upon with unseemly haste. Archaeological contractors have been hired for short periods and under time pressures that forced them to accept unrealistic deadlines. As the journal *British Archaeology* reported, BAA set out to change that:

> 'Imagine this', said Richard Morris, former Director of the Council for British Archaeology. 'A public limited company embarks upon a development project on land which is archeologically fertile. The company recognises the value of the archaeology, approaches it in a responsible manner, and when their archaeological consultants come up with an imaginative research strategy, they welcome it. Utopian fantasy? No, the company is BAA plc.'

The company had hired an archaeological contractor with whom it could build a long-term trusting relationship. Together company and contractor set out to reverse the usual approach to archeology: instead of 'bolt it on at the back', the strategy became 'plan it up front'. BAA asked the contractor to set objectives, and funded academic research to develop a methodology for meeting them in advance of the fieldwork. The company also demanded rigorous monitoring and benchmarking during the fieldwork, which enabled the development of predictive models that have allowed workflows to be planned with confidence, reducing the risk.

The basic philosophy of the approach to archaeology shifted. Traditionally the main thrust of archaeological analysis takes place after fieldwork is complete. On-site material is slavishly recorded, and interpretation – an understanding of what it all means – is largely deferred until later. The T5 approach involved more investigation in the field, with contractors achieving a wider perspective early on and then homing in on evidence that tells the real story. Computer-based on-site recording and analysis enabled the material to be interpreted during excavation so that the work could be re-directed where necessary. The focus was not on recording and describing objects and deposits, but on writing the history of the area. The result is not just a more interesting archaeological 'product', but also a 20 per cent reduction in costs per hectare, largely because analysis is undertaken on-site allowing resources to be clearly focused on meeting the project's objectives. Gill Andrews, BAA's Archaeological Consultant for the T5 project, summed up the new approach:

> The T5 philosophy represents a paradigm shift in the way companies and archaeological contractors go about archaeology. BAA has set an important precedent in devising and implementing its own archaeological policy. This policy demands that all work is carried out in accordance with best practice and that there is a commitment to make the results of that work available to a wide public.

There has been widespread support within the archaeological profession for the developments that BAA has initiated. English Heritage has said:

> the archaeology of the (T5) site will be treated in an exemplary manner, using the latest investigative techniques and interpretative approaches.... BAA would appear to have taken a positive and progressive role to their responsibilities in regard to the buried heritage that we can welcome.

It is intended that finds and other material from the excavations will be housed in the Museum of London. The knowledge gained will also be included in a display at the Heathrow Visitor Centre and will be shared through a variety of different media with schools and the wider community.

All this and a financial saving to the company. It has to make sense.

Summary: The Answer is in the Detail

If the sheer volume of detail in this chapter has stretched your patience, we understand. There are those who find it convenient to their cause never to give credit to BAA, and one of their charges is that Contract with the Community is 'just PR'. We believe this chapter gives the lie to that. The scope of the programme speaks for itself. Few companies anywhere in the world can claim to do so much.

Where will the company go from here? We know that Mike Hodgkinson is committed to its ideals, not least because he has seen the benefits. Likewise the new generation of airport managers. And we know the Board of BAA has chosen as Group Airports Director and Mike's eventual successor Mike Clasper, who has already been honoured for his contribution to corporate environmental responsibility. This is all encouraging, but the real guarantee of the sustainability of this approach lies, first, in training and internal educational programmes to embed it as a core belief and set of skills at every level of the company; second, in the business benefits it brings to the company, for the more corporate responsibility is seen to contribute to the growth and profitability of the business, the more committed everyone will be; and, third, in the management systems, processes and audited reports that place it, and pin it to the heart of the business.

Contract with the Community is about practical response to practical problems, about balancing negatives with positives, about a way of working that seeks to meet the needs of the company's community and social stakeholders. Has it further to go? Of course. This has been a new experience and all the better for being developed within the company. It has been a genuine learning experience. But is it a good start by a company dedicated to doing the right thing? We believe so.

Part III

So You Want to Be a Stakeholder Company?

CHAPTER 5

Corporate Citizenship
Six Key Points – Three Key Players

Key 1: Avoid Cosmetic Solutions

There is a story we like about the chairman of a chemical company in the US whose office overlooked a beautiful lake. He so liked the view that he ordered his PR director to take a photograph from his window. When the PR director arrived with the photo the chairman noticed a red smudge on the water. 'What's this?' he asked.

The PR director looked embarrassed. 'Well actually, sir,' he replied, 'you're looking at our chemicals in the water. You can't see them with the naked eye but the camera has picked them up.'

The chairman was horrified. 'This is terrible', he said. 'Go and find out what we can do about it.'

Three days later the PR director was back with the photograph. The red smudge had been carefully edited out.

That was his idea of 'doing something about it'.

One of the main allegations made by those who are sceptical of the move to social responsibility is that companies are really only engaging in a public relations exercise, that it is all spin and no substance, that the approach is cosmetic rather than providing real solutions to real problems. One of the better-known (albeit one of the sillier) UK environmentalists wrote recently of the 'smoke and mirrors of PR, along with complex environmental policies and reports ... duping the public into believing positive change is under way'.

The charge that corporate citizenship, corporate social responsibility and stakeholderism are a PR invention is one its advocates have to answer. Because there is some truth in it. There are companies that believe a bit of philanthropy is all that is needed to smooth the path to their objectives. There are others that believe making a few gestures to social responsibility can cover up the real environmental and social impact of their business.

There are those who believe high-minded rhetoric or glossy publications will do the trick. Yes, there are those whose claims to corporate citizenship can only be described as downright cynical. Who, for instance, could be persuaded by tobacco companies like the one that recently placed a series of corporate advertisements in magazines such as the *New Statesman,* claiming to sell cigarettes 'with a demonstrated sense of responsibility and responsiveness to the issues surrounding smoking and health.... [We are] committed to being a good corporate citizen'? (It even had the gall to advertise – we repeat, advertise – that it 'supports a wide range of charities without seeking public recognition or reward'.)

Scepticism about how genuine many companies are has been most effectively voiced recently by Naomi Klein in *No Logo.* She paints a picture of companies producing largely PR-orientated codes of conduct or action programmes in answer to criticism.

Well, yes, we have acknowledged that sceptics have a point, but they don't help their cause by not acknowledging the huge change that has taken place in business thinking, and the number of companies that are trying hard to do the right thing. For instance, how many readers who have just completed the previous chapter had an inkling of the scope of BAA's stakeholder activities? We suspect the answer is only a handful. That is partly because good news is not news and rarely gets a fair airing, but also because anti-business groups will never acknowledge either good intentions or good activity because they do not fit the picture they need to paint to achieve their purpose.

The fact is that progressive companies know only too well that ethical posturing or cosmetic solutions won't wash: that articulate and well-educated neighbours and highly professional special interest groups are too well-informed and intelligent to be fooled by so-called 'solutions' that will not work. They know that effective campaigners can use exaggerated claims to their advantage. There is clear warning in *No Logo.*

> One [approach] that has become increasingly popular is throwing the promises in the code of conduct back in the faces of the corporations who drafted them ... it's the Saul Alinsky theory of political jujitsu: 'No organisation can live up to the letter of its own book. You can club them to death with their book of rules and regulations.'

Klein quotes another campaigner talking about Nike:

Let's face it, hypocrites are far more interesting than mere wrong-doers, and it's been much easier to sensitize press and public to Nike's failure to implement its own code of conduct than to its failure to comply with Indonesian labour law.

The message is clear: create a cosmetic programme and make exaggerated claims, or introduce a code of conduct you have no real intention of observing, and you will be hit over the head with your own words. (This, incidentally, is why BAA is careful to distinguish in promoting sustainability between what it can itself do and what it can only advocate; likewise on T5, for instance, while it could ask that a third Heathrow runway be ruled out, it could not make a precise promise because ultimately the decision was not the company's alone.)

Apart from the external sceptics, however, there is another group the company has to be particularly sensitive to, namely its employees, who will not be fooled by lies and yet whose wholehearted support is vital. There is no more effective way to engender cynicism in a workforce, or fail to inspire them to work for process improvement and greater productivity, than by insulting their intelligence with internal and external claims about company behaviour or ethics that employees know to be false.

So our first advice to any company seeking to be part of the twenty-first century business revolution and to join the ranks of the socially responsible is: forget it unless the company is genuinely committed, not only to the concept of social responsibility but also to identifying the real stakeholder issues and tackling them in a way that will make a real difference.

There may, of course, remain differences between the company and some of its critics. BAA, for instance, knows that there are some who believe that aviation activity at existing levels, let alone predicted levels, is unsustainable because of its use of energy and possible, albeit unproven, environmental effects. As is obvious, BAA does not share that view. It believes that the overall environmental effect is not so damaging that the need to address it outweighs the economic and social case for growth. More critically, however, it believes that the industry is capable of finding ways of making the industry sustainable. The fact is that the debate between the extremes of the environmental movement and BAA may never be reconcilable, but what matters is, first, that the company does what it believes to be right, and, second, that it tries to find reasonable common ground with reasonable people. BAA also knows that few companies can make their industry sustainable on their own; hence current Chief Executive Mike Hodgkinson's campaign throughout the industry to encourage aircraft manufacturers to invest in the kind of technology that will reduce energy use and lead to quieter planes. By engaging in this he acknowledges that these goals are not within BAA's power to achieve.

One of the main charges against multinational companies is that they adopt reasonably creditable social-responsibility and sustainability policies in industrialised countries such as the UK or the US, only to abandon them in Third World countries. Or that they block or contest internationally desirable environmental or social advances by use of their lobbying muscle. Their influence over the Bush Administration over the Kyoto proposals is heavily criticised. This is a charge that has some substance. As we argue in the next chapter, these double standards are not even self-serving in the longer term.

We cannot stress too strongly, however, that those companies that adopt any of the concepts we advocate – corporate social responsibility, corporate citizenship, stakeholderism or sustainability – for PR reasons, with no desire to embrace them genuinely, will not only fail but do a serious disservice to business as a whole. They will breed cynicism, first about their own company, then about business and industry generally.

Any chief executive or board confronted with programmes in this area should ask the questions: whose are the concerns we're confronting? And what are the concerns we're confronting? Will what is proposed address those concerns realistically and make us the solution rather than the problem? Or is it designed merely to achieve temporary relief from criticism, to buy us time, or make us look good to other stakeholders? If the latter is so, how long will the benefits last and what will be the ultimate price we pay in cynicism and damage to our reputation and brand?

As for making promises the company has no intention of keeping, this can only lead to a loss of trust that will bedevil relationships for evermore. In the long term it will probably make no difference in any case, because the company will be made to do what it should have done, but on a regulator's terms instead of its own.

Writing in the *Observer* recently, the chairman of Rio Tinto, Sir Robert Wilson, said:

> A pressing concern for the mining industry is the need to overcome poor public perceptions of our industry's [environmental] performance and our consequent growing vulnerability to increased

regulation based not on scientific analysis but popular prejudice....
The sector made attempts to balance these perceptions with public
relations campaigns, advertising and educational programmes. But
this sort of response achieved very little. It was time for a rethink.
This is what prompted a meeting of the chairmen and chief executives from 10 major international companies – crucial was a
willingness by the company leaders to acknowledge that the
industry had a case to answer in terms of its economic, environmental and social performance. We should not try to sway public
opinion but rather to accept we have made mistakes and to actively
engage with, and listen to our critics, to help us to try to define
priority areas to try to improve performance.

He then went on to describe a major industry initiative to find a new way to
grow. He accepted that the growth would bring balancing down and
upsides, but was setting out how a whole industry was abandoning a
cosmetic approach to criticism and trying to find real answers to real
problems. We can but wish him and his colleagues well.

In the final analysis we are discussing what a company is all about. What
does it exist for? What are its values? There may be a few companies that
can afford to think in terms of the bottom line alone, but they most definitely are not those operating at the interface between the public and
private sectors, as more and more companies do. Before companies like
BAA were privatised, they were publicly owned services. They existed not
to make a profit, but to serve the nation: in the case of BAA, by providing
the country with efficient and impressive gateways in the form of airports.
They were not privatised just to create profitable companies for shareholders; they were privatised because it was believed that with private
enterprise incentives they would perform their public service even better. In
some cases whether that has been achieved is debatable, as in the case of
Railtrack. But BAA can claim to have combined the best traditions of
public service with the more positive characteristics of private enterprise.
It is not just about profit; its mission statement says it is about providing the
UK with the best airports in the world, about safety and security, about
customer service, and about caring for its neighbours. The profits come
because it does all this well. If profits are falling and there is pressure from
the City, a company like BAA may well from time to time have to take
defensive financial measures such as cutting costs, but we believe those cuts

would never be at the expense of those fundamental mission statement objectives. They would not be sought by any measures that sacrificed the highest safety standards, nor by letting customers down, nor by harming neighbours. Any neglect of these stakeholders would lead the company into a downward spiral and probably to tough action by its regulator, perhaps even in the form of breakup of its ownership of the UK's leading airports.

The fact is that BAA has proved that if you serve your customers well, grow your facilities as their numbers grow, change as they indicate what it is they want, and put their comfort and safety first, the profits follow.

In their book *Built to Last*, James C. Collins and Jerry Porras write about Merck, the US company that decided to give away a drug to cure river blindness because their 'customers' in the Third World could not afford it. They argue that for all the idealism of that act, Merck always combined 'high ideals and pragmatic self interest'. They quote George Merck II:

> I want ... to express the principles which we in our company have endeavoured to live up to.... We try to remember that medicine is for the patient. We try never to forget that medicine is for the people. It is not for the profits. The profits follow, and if we have remembered that, they have never failed to appear. The better we have remembered it, the larger they have been.

We will return to this issue of profit in the next chapter, but for now let's ask not whether 'doing the right thing' reduces profit, but rather whether pretending to do the right thing enhances it. This we doubt. It may bring some short-term benefit, but in the end the anger, cynicism or rejection by stakeholders becomes all the greater. Corporate citizenship – stakeholderism – is not about gestures. It is not about minor concessions, grudgingly made then over-promoted. It is about deciding to be a better company, changing accordingly, and honouring the stake in the business that every stakeholder has.

Finally, on this subject, we should address the question of company charity giving and philanthropy, and whether this is in itself enough. There may be some companies who have no direct effect on the community that they need to balance and for which becoming members of the One Per Cent Club is at least one practical step they can take. Others, like BAA, create a charity as a way to make a specific contribution to their community stakeholders. But it is our experience that a company's citizenship responsibilities and/or its obligations to its stakeholders will not usually be met just by donating to good causes. Rather we are impressed by the comment of a senior executive of Timberland interviewed at a 1997 Danish conference:

> We perceive and deal with social issues in a nontraditional manner.... We don't give money to charity. Instead we try to create a return. We integrate the notion of value creation into all of our activities. We create values for ourselves as a company, our employees, our shareholders, our customers, the community, and the non-profitmaking organisations we cooperate with. The traditional notion of philanthropy is not adequate. It is not smart or wise to approach the social problems of society with the financial left-overs of companies. By integrating our social activities into our business strategies we also provide those social activities with the sustainability that will see them through hard times, and harness business to work in another fashion.

This last point is crucial: the only way that a stakeholder approach can be assured of sustainability is if it is integrated into the core business objectives and strategy in a way that does not make it vulnerable to the cost accountant's knife. Only by being universally accepted within the company as fundamental to its approach and essential to the achievements of all its goals will it be secure.

Key 2: Adopt a Reasonable Approach To Pressure Groups

This brings us to pressure groups. We do not share the view that these groups are undemocratic and, by definition, enemies of business to be defeated at all costs. The right of citizens to fight for their interests is a fundamental feature of democracy. The voluntary sector in the UK has an honourable tradition of promoting positive change. Pressure groups often identify genuine problems and promote solutions that the political 'system' has missed or – for one reason or another – gives little priority to. One of the authors of this book, Des Wilson, has a history of involvement in pressure groups – with Shelter, CLEAR, Friends of the Earth, the Campaign for Freedom of Information, and others – and believes passionately in their right to exist. He would argue from a basis of real achievement that they can be a major force for good.

We believe, therefore, that those companies that assume all pressure groups are destructive trouble-makers are wrong: wrong in their denial of the groups' right to exist, usually wrong in their assumptions about the groups' motivations, and wrong in the way they respond to them.

Our view is that the company should always be available to listen to and talk to citizen groups, always ready to share information and views, and, above all, always looking for the common ground. After all, if you are going to have a fight, at least reduce the ground you are fighting on, and make sure that you have tried all reasonable ways to resolve differences. This is less expensive in financial and reputation terms. And it is the right thing to do as one citizen in a democratic process shared with others.

By respecting the right of the individual or the group to exist and be heard, companies will find there are prizes to be won. For instance, even the opponents at the T5 inquiry, dedicated to stopping the airport's growth, joined in the local Transport Forum. Special interest groups belong to the kind of airport consultative committee that helped produce an outstanding result for BAA at Gatwick. By identifying common ground and working together, companies and the more constructive citizen groups can help each other to achieve their respective objectives in the most acceptable way.

NGOs, citizen groups, pressure groups, call them what you like, vary enormously, from small groups of local citizens fighting for a particular local cause to national and even international movements like Friends of the Earth or Greenpeace, who may fight on specific issues but usually within a wider cause, in their case the environmental cause. In most cases they have lost faith in legislators to deliver their objectives; their aim is to exert 'pressure' on whoever has the power – whether it be company, local council, or national government – to force them to listen and to act. This is their right. Where they become controversial is in the means they adopt to fight their corner. Some do so by high-quality research and argument. We single out Maurice Frankel and the Campaign for Freedom of Information as a classic operator in this. Some do so by imaginative publicity stunts. Some by disruption or breaking the law. It is not our purpose to make judgements here. We prefer simply to say that we defend the right of these groups to act in any way that is reasonable, especially if they themselves are open to reason. And we urge business to fight their corner with reason. Both sides have much to learn from each other.

But what about the unreasonable? The ones that refuse to enter into dialogue with the company? The 'punk campaigners' who rarely bother

with fact, are not interested in compromise, who trade in abuse and unpro-
ductive demonstrations rather than put the work into trying to achieve a
reasonable response to reasonable concerns? Then we take the view the
company has every right to argue its case forcefully and, where it has the
opportunity and the case to defend itself from lawless action by use of the
law, to do so. Even in such cases, though, the company should fight the
unreasonable reasonably. There is no better indicator of where right lies
than in the behaviour of the advocates in the dispute; those who argue and
behave reasonably, especially in the face of lack of reason, are far more
likely to be persuasive.

If we have a regret about the behaviour of too many citizen groups, it is
about their rejection of compromise. It is disillusioning for those in business
and industry who are working hard to change their companies, who seek
dialogue with all who can contribute, and who can show real gains for the
causes the citizen groups claim to espouse, if no matter what they do they
are attacked, their motives questioned, their improvements minimised, their
good intentions rejected. This discourages the best in business and makes
it more difficult for them to persuade their colleagues. The best of the environmental movement, people like Jonathon Porritt and John Elkington and
Paul Ekins, know this. They do not pretend that working with business has
always been easy. But equally they know that it offers the best chance of
real results.

Only the more mindless anti-business campaigners can really deny that
the answer to the overwhelming majority of economic and environmental
problems facing the world lies with business and industry; only they can
generate the wealth necessary to alleviate poverty without reducing the
qualify of life achieved by the majority in the developed world; only they
have the resources to create technical routes to sustainability. Perhaps only
world-class companies know just what potential for good world-class
companies can offer, but if they are to be motivated to realise that potential
they need encouragement, not constant denigration no matter what they do.

On the day the Heathrow Express was launched, Friends of the Earth International were meeting in Manchester. BAA asked them if they would like to
make a welcoming comment; after all, FoE had campaigned for more public
transport for years and this was the first new major rail service since the
Second World War. This was a chance for the environmental group to
encourage a company doing the right thing and show that it was capable of
being positive when positive things happened. Instead it could not resist

combining a half-hearted response with a sideswipe at the aviation industry. This did little to improve communication where communication was needed, or to encourage those who were campaigning within BAA for more public transport initiatives. And the irony was that the overwhelming majority at this international conference had, of course, travelled to it by plane!

Key 3: Leadership Must Come From The Top ... But There Are Three Key Players

Ironically, some of the opponents of social responsibility will be found within the company itself.

As the BAA experience shows an effective social responsibility programme calls for many contributors and ultimately the involvement of everyone in the company, but three people are particularly well placed to give leadership.

The Chief Executive

By far the most important is the chief executive. While he (or she) can and should delegate much to the team of top managers, he cannot delegate responsibility for setting the tone; the company's ethical culture has to be established from the top. Indeed when it comes to the culture of the company he has to be more than a leader, he has to be a campaigner within his own company, driving home the message, whether it be the importance of customer service or environmental responsibility.

BAA had a programme called Sharing the Vision. Every week a small group of young managers would go to the company's training centre near Gatwick for a few days to learn about the company's objectives and values and to be encouraged, as the course title suggests, to share the vision of its leadership. John Egan went to considerable lengths never to miss a group, usually going down in the evening to talk to and have dinner with the group. He was determined they should know that he shared the vision with his managers. But he also went to listen, to find out whether people were living by the mission statement in every part of the company the managers came from.

These days it has become fashionable to question the value of mission statements. John is a strong supporter of them. In a paper on leadership, he wrote:

The mission statement is about direction and strategy, but it is also about effective involvement of employees at every level. The best business leaders know that it enhances the performance of their company if their employees bring their enthusiasm and intelligence to work as well as their hands and feet. Involving your employees in a way that realises their full potential also generates a considerable additional wave of energy and directing this energy into common purpose is one of the key goals of the leader.

Leadership starts with a vision of where the company could go … what is possible with the resources the company has or can acquire. The mission statement is, or should be much more than high-sounding rhetoric. It should be a practical document that sets out a detailed set of goals and the rules that will apply to achieving them. And it should be created by, debated, and finalised by the full management team and only changed by the full management team so that there is genuine commitment. It should then be explained throughout the company.

When in doubt as to what to do, the first step any employee should take is to look to the mission statement for the solution. If their actions are consistent with that, it's unlikely they'll make a major mistake.

Given the importance placed on the mission statement, it was therefore vital that it should have Contract with the Community at its heart. John played a major part in leading the debate over the change in the mission statement to incorporate it. It took nearly a year to achieve one line in the mission statement: 'we will grow with the trust and support of our neighbours'. Why? Because John would not incorporate it until he was convinced he had the level of buy-in to ensure the promise was kept – especially after he was gone. He asked every member of his executive committee, the management group that ran the company, to undertake a specific leadership role within the programme.

Charles Dunstone of Carphone Warehouse is another chief executive who believes in leading from the front, especially when it comes to that crucial stakeholder, the customer. In an article he wrote:

Maybe there is more of a sense now that the person at the top of the business has to be accountable to the customers. I give customers my personal e-mail and direct line so they can speak to me because I think that's really important. Not just important to the customers but as a signal to everyone in the organisation that we're in this together. We're all accountable when something goes wrong, whether or not it's our fault, and we've got to resolve it together.

The responsibility goes beyond the chief executive to the whole board. It can be totally destructive if the chief executive is advocating social responsibility while other board members are expressing scepticism. The chief executive must convince himself that he has the full understanding and support of the board before he rolls the thinking out. Time needs to be taken at board meetings and strategy away-days to debate the issues with the same care and attention as any other company affairs. This is about the core of the company – its beliefs and values and relationships with all its stakeholders – and if it is not getting board attention you have to ask why.

The chief executive has also to take care to ensure that his leadership is backed up by organisation, by a process that delivers.

If any chief executive thinks this is going to be easy, he or she should consider the characteristics of the new breed of 'Citizen COs' suggested by John Elkington in his recent book *The Chrysalis Economy*:

- a strong vision
- an acute sense of commercial and political timing
- the survival skills and stamina to pursue [this] agenda through the inevitable market squalls and storms
- well-developed peripheral vision – coupled with a real concern for (and capacity to manage) multiple forms of capital
- an appreciation of diversity in all its forms
- unusual sensitivity to the full range of past, present and potential future impacts caused by the company and its value web
- the wisdom to create a culture of openness, honesty and constructive criticism
- a readiness to walk the talk, adapting the business not just in compliance with the relevant laws and regulations, but also in response to emerging voluntary standards and societal values
- an honest assessment of – and willingness to admit to – gaps in his or her understanding and performance, and a determination to remedy them
- a genuine, inclusive desire to learn from others, inside and outside the company

- more specifically, the capacity to learn from the inevitable failures – and to help others to do likewise
- effective networking across his or her sector, and across the wider business community, with a particular focus on enlightening the darker corners of the financial world
- a capacity to integrate triple bottom line thinking, targets and perform-ance from the boardroom to the workplace
- a willingness to believe that zero (e.g. accidents, health risks, waste, environmental impacts) is both desirable and achievable – and a deter-mination to drive the business in this direction
- a passion to identify, invest in and incubate more sustainable products, technologies, services and business models
- a recognition that sustainability is a journey, not a destination
- an interest in legacy
- a healthy sense of humour
- and luck.

Corporate and Public Affairs Director

Another key player is the director of corporate and public affairs, because he or she controls the channels of communication, both internally and extern-ally. In fact he (or she) may have one of many titles: PR director, director of corporate communications, and so on. But at BAA he was Des Wilson, and he was called Director of Corporate and Public Affairs, a title reflecting two very different areas of responsibility: first, to represent BAA, a private sector company, to its business and financial stakeholders; but, second, to represent BAA, custodian of national infrastructure and the keeper of the national gateways, to its public stakeholders.

In the old days the holders of these posts were often old company management retainers, past their best but not deserving of being ignomin-iously put out to grass. 'Why not put old Jim in charge of PR?' the board would say, giving him an office with a cocktail cabinet and a generous expense account. The caricature was a portly man with a bow tie who after spending the morning constructing a subsequently unpublished press release would leave for a three-hour lunch with a journalist, staggering back afterwards reeking of alcohol.

These days journalists have no time for a lengthy lunch, and usually these encounters are drink-free. And the director of CPA – who may still, alas, like Des be portly – is now more likely to be an experienced communications professional leading a multi-disciplined team and representing it on the company's executive or management committee, where he or she shares in developing the policy of the whole company and has a key role advising on the company's positioning and relationships. The real title could easily be director of stakeholder relationships, except that would be wrong because stakeholder relationships are, as we made clear earlier in this chapter, the responsibility of everybody, starting with the chief executive.

In the old days, CPA directors would have been communicating outwards, their duty to convey the company line, to publicise its activities or sell its story and, if necessary, to cover up its mistakes or bad behaviour. It was not their role to influence company policy, but to defend, explain or promote it. They were messengers, and sometimes placators or even seducers. If they were good at what they did, they were paid reasonably well, but were rarely respected either inside or outside the company.

In Chapter 1 we described the campaign for lead-free petrol. The behaviour of the petroleum industry PR men was typical of these old-style operators. Confronted with the crisis facing their companies, namely a public confrontation with the environmental movement in the form of Des Wilson's CLEAR campaign, they never attempted to establish the facts, or if they did it was only to misrepresent them. Nor did they ever attempt to persuade their masters that the message they were being asked to convey was not only a fraud but one that would do the companies more harm than good.

They produced glossy brochures quoting only the scientific 'evidence' of their own industrial scientists or one or two others who shared their views. Most of their material ignored the evidence of harmful effects altogether, not even attempting to answer it. They exaggerated the difficulties and cost of removing lead from petrol. They questioned the motives of their opponents. Their message was that leaded petrol was harmless and that the environmentalists were emotive and hysterical. It could only be eliminated at huge cost to both the industry and the motorist. Above all they advised their employers not to meet the campaigners and not to answer their questions.

Let us look at how they could have behaved.

When the first questions were raised they should have urged their companies to pay for objective research to establish the facts. This would have revealed that there was growing evidence of a health risk. Also that other countries were already acting upon it and getting real results. In the US, for instance, the amount of lead in petrol had been reduced by 55 per cent and research had shown that lead in blood in the US population had fallen 37 per cent. They would have established that the Japanese and the Australians were also moving to lead-free petrol. They would have established that it could be removed at less cost than was being suggested. They would at the very least have suggested to their employers that there was a world-wide trend towards lead-free petrol, based on genuine concerns, and that therefore the issue had to be taken seriously. Had they given this advice, and insisted it be listened to, the industry could have handled the whole issue with much more care and probably have avoided the humiliations that were to follow.

Second, they should have urged their companies to meet the people who had initially written to them. 'All these people are in *Who's Who*', they should have said. 'They're influential and they've demonstrated their ability to capture public attention. We can't ignore them. We must at least treat them with respect, listen to them, give them our side of the story, see if we can find some common ground.' By ignoring Des Wilson and others they merely raised further suspicions, for surely, the campaigners thought, they must have something to hide. Furthermore they forced the debate into the public arena. When later they complained about CLEAR's 'confrontational tactics', CLEAR was able to reply: 'We tried to talk to you, you wouldn't listen; we asked questions, you wouldn't answer; you pushed this into the public arena, not us.'

Above all the PR men should have told their companies 'the days when you can just brush aside public concerns on health and safety are gone. You have to take them seriously. And that means convincing yourselves that the concerns are not justified, because if they are the campaigners are likely to win. We should do the right thing and tackle the real problem, not just the PR problem.'

Compare the PR men for the petroleum and lead additive industry (and later the paint manufacturers who, even after seeing what happened on lead in petrol, sought fruitlessly to resist calls to take lead out of paint) with the food can manufacturers. One of the biggest food can manufacturers had a sensible corporate affairs director who came to the CLEAR campaign and said:

Look, we've been listening to you. We use lead in the solder of food cans; we had no idea that at these low levels it could threaten children's health. We're prepared to act voluntarily to eliminate it. If we announce this and do so over a reasonable timescale that doesn't harm our business, will you cooperate with us rather than criticise.

CLEAR was only too pleased to cooperate and the food can industry eliminated lead from solder without one bad headline and over a period of time that worked for them.

The corporate and public affairs director who believes his role is to tell his company only what it wants to hear is worthless. He should not only be the company's voice to the outside world, but the voice of the outside world to the company. He should ensure that the company's communication with its stakeholders is not a monologue but a dialogue. He should ensure that research is conducted to establish the truth, not just to prove a case (especially one that may be weak or dishonest). He should be the conscience of the company, always asking 'but is this right?', 'are we treating our stakeholders properly?'

He should argue for the long term. 'Yes, it could cost the company to take swift action to make a product safer, or to reduce pollution, but usually it is less expensive in financial and reputation terms to do what has to be done now, rather than be pushed into doing it in the full glare of the public spotlight and at greater expense later.'

The CPA director is not the guardian of the company's worst secrets, he is the watchdog over its behaviour. At all times he must drive home, in the words of US journalist-campaigner Sam Smith, that the best PR is to do the right thing.

At the same time he must understand that if the company is going to be a genuine stakeholder company, the ultimate responsibility cannot and must not rest with him. Corporate citizenship is not about PR. It is about what the company really is – about its real and underlying values.

Thus while Des Wilson played a vital role in BAA in driving forward the idea of Contract with the Community, mobilising supporters within the company, and developing a plan for how it could be developed, he always understood that the only chance of success was if the policy was owned, first, by the chief executive, then, second, by the management at every level, but above all at the level where day-by-day decisions were taken. That was why we sought out a tough airport managing director to chair the

Contract with the Community Board, and a long-time airport manager to be first community relations director: because they knew the business, understood the pressures on their colleagues, and had the credibility.

The CPA director may often be the originator of a corporate citizenship approach for three reasons. First, if he is properly in tune with the world outside the company (and that is his job), he should know what the stakeholders are thinking and saying and wanting. Second, he is often able to stand aside from the day-to-day operations and better see how the company is positioned in relation to its stakeholders and how it can be positioned. Third, he should be a professional communicator, in charge of the company's communications channels, and thus be able to give the change real impetus by keeping it in the forefront of company thinking and not allowing any initial enthusiasm to die.

He should also be a trusted advisor to the chief executive and be well placed to see that the concept is kept at the top of his or her agenda. Finally, as the manager of what should be two-way communications, the CPA director can ensure that stakeholders feed into the process and wherever possible participate in it.

Corporate and public affairs is, therefore, central to corporate citizenship: as advocate within the company, as facilitator of relationships, as communicator. But ultimately the concept must belong to the mainstream management.

At BAA, Des Wilson was the innovator and driving force at first; by the time he left, he was not even attending the Contract with the Community Board. The responsibility for corporate citizenship had been absorbed by the mainstream management. He was particularly proud of that.

Community Relations or Social Responsibility Director

The third key player is the community relations or social responsibility director – or perhaps the title should be 'stakeholder affairs director'; it depends on the company. Given that the chief executive has to be taking an overview of all aspects of the company's affairs and the director of corporate and public affairs also has a wider role – the first responsible for overall leadership of the programme and the second for its communication – that leaves the need for someone to take the responsibility for day-to-day coordination and management of programmes. While this should be overseen by a project

board, there is still in our view an overwhelming case for having one individual who is accountable for driving the programme forward, coordinating
every aspect of it, representing it on training programmes, and at internal
conferences and events, administering its funds, acting as chief executive of
the company's charity if it has one, and so on. At BAA this was Chris Hoare
(it is now Andrew Currie). He was under no illusion that he had to become a
campaigner within the company and offers these six pieces of advice to a
would-be community relations director:

> First, never stop fighting the corner.... Identify the driving forces
> in your organisation and also the barriers to change. This means
> really knowing your organisation, who works in it, what motivates
> them, and being ready to engage in dialogue and debate.
>
> Second, concentrate on awareness-creation and communica-
> tion within the organisation before you consider going outside. We
> were in the third year of Contract with the Community before we
> began to communicate externally. Use conventional and uncon-
> ventional communications channels with a consistent message and
> memorable theme.
>
> Third, never let the chief executive or board off the hook.
> Keep them actively on side. They're under a lot of conflicting
> pressures; your task is to never let them forget their leadership
> role in this area.
>
> Fourth, don't expect instant results. If the forces for the status
> quo were believers, there would be no need for change. You have
> to win their hearts and minds before you can get the commitment
> of resources and consistent support you need.
>
> Fifth, make your first target the mission statement and corpor-
> ate plan. This has to be at the core of the business.
>
> Sixth, link up with colleagues in other companies. There's an
> overwhelming business case for what you're doing, and their expe-
> riences can help you make it.

These then are three key players. But their importance should not be
allowed to over-ride the fact that for a corporate citizenship or stakeholder
programme to really work it must engage everybody in the company:
board, managers, employees, acting together, all sharers in a vision of a
company they can be proud of.

Key 4: It Is Not Just About Money

When first confronted with the challenge to become more socially responsible, many companies assume they are looking at having to invest considerable sums of money. Indeed this is sometimes the most practical thing a
company can do. Many belong to the One Per Cent Club, a group of companies that commit themselves to invest at least one per cent of their profits
before tax to good causes. But as we have already argued, straight donations
of money, or even expensive projects, are by no means the only options. This
does not have to be about money, at least not in the first instance.

When it comes to the local community, the first and most important
contribution a company can make is to cease those actions that cause
concern to their stakeholders. In other words, if you are polluting their air
or water, stop. And if it is not within your power to do this, try to balance
your impacts. Thus while BAA cannot eradicate aircraft noise, it can take
a variety of steps to mitigate its effects and can (and does) ensure that fines
for airlines contravening noise agreements are spent in the communities
they affect. Many of the most effective measures or counter-balances cost
no money at all.

The second possible contribution is to make a creative input to solving
other local problems. Company leaders can similarly contribute to national
and regional activity. John Egan at BAA led the drive for a change in the
way the construction industry works. As a result he was asked by John
Prescott, the Deputy Prime Minister, to head up a task force to drive the
changes across the whole industry; its report 'Rethinking Construction' has
been hugely influential. He also chaired the Central London Partnership
and the London Tourist Board and was active in a number of other industry
bodies. His successor, Mike Hodgkinson, serves on the board of the
London Transport Authority. Janis Kong, while in charge of Gatwick, has
served on the regional development authority for her area. Many other
managers make a similar contribution, the company encouraging managers
to become school governors or to undertake other community activities.
This is not about money; it is about time and energy, and it too brings its
rewards in more rounded managers who are learning from the experience,
and the experiences of the community around it.

The drive for conservation of resources and environmental sustainability
may add to company costs; equally it may reduce them. For instance,
energy conservation saves energy costs.

Ethical standards, respect for human rights, fair employment policies, proper treatment of small suppliers are rarely costly to a company; if they do cost money, it is more than possible this is because the company has been making its profits at an unacceptable expense.

In their book *Everybody's Business*, David Grayson and Adrian Hodges identify what they call 'the seven Ps of corporate contribution'. These are:

- **Product:** the contribution to community organisations of products or services, perhaps products that are usable but for one reason or another no longer appropriate for the market, or equipment that is no longer useful for the business (for example, a company updating its computers can donate the redundant ones to voluntary organisations who do not need the latest technology and would be only too pleased to have them).
- **Premises:** provision of free accommodation for NGOs and access to business premises out of hours. (BAA, for instance, 'let' its Victoria conference room free of charge to London voluntary organisations, saving them paying out hard-earned funds on conference facilities; Carphone Warehouse houses the whole Get Connected helpline in its corporate resource centre – and pays for the phone calls).
- **Purchasing:** the use of purchasing power to achieve social goals, for example by buying a proportion of products or services from local concerns or minority groups.
- **Power:** empowering local organisations with educational help or other opportunities, and using the company's influence to open doors to sources of aid.
- **Promotion:** undertaking cause-related campaigns to promote a social cause (for example, Carphone Warehouse's promotion of the Get Connected help-line for runaways).
- **People:** mobilising the expertise and time of professionals to contribute to local community activity.
- **Profit:** investing money in community activity (for instance, the BAA's three Es charity for environmental, employment and educational activity around its airports).

We are not, of course, saying that a company should not invest money to be an effective corporate citizen and servant of its stakeholders. Sometimes what it has to do can be expensive, as in the case of many of BAA's public transport initiatives, but then if this is about a licence to grow the business, that spending makes financial sense. What we are saying is that corporate citizenship is not necessarily about money; just as the values of an individual are reflected in many ways, by what he or she does or says, as well as spends, so it is with a company.

Key 5: Look for the Synergies

By far the most effective corporate citizenship or stakeholder campaigns are those that are synergistic with the business. When outsiders take note of the project they should not find themselves asking 'why is that company doing that?' It should be obvious. If it is obvious then the company is probably relating its CSR activities to its product or services, and thus to its stakeholders: 'integrating its social activities into its business strategies', to quote that Timberland executive to whom we referred earlier.

A classic case of synergy is mobile phone retailer Carphone Warehouse's partnership with the charity Get Connected. Every year a substantial number of young people run away from home, sometimes for just a day or so, sometimes for longer. According to the National Children's Society, 100 000 under-16s run away from home every year. One in seven will be hurt. Of those taken in by a stranger, half will be physically or sexually abused. Get Connected was set up in 1999 to reduce the risk of physical and emotional damage to these youngsters by providing them with a free phone number – a helpline – to trained volunteers who will respond in a way they can trust and connect them to the best service to advise, help and support in each individual case. It handled 1000 calls in its first year, 6000 in its second, and expects to reach 30 000 within a year or so.

The synergies between Get Connected and Carphone Warehouse (CPW) were, first, that there was a clear relationship between the charity and the company's product: the telephone. Second, the vulnerable age group – young people – related to CPW's biggest customer base. Third, CPW's slogan – simple, impartial advice – was a perfect description of what Get Connected offered.

So CPW entered into a unique partnership with Get Connected to build up the volunteer base, and thus the quality and scope of the service, and to market the helpline number to the young. The company moved the charity lock, stock and barrel into purpose-built facilities at its main national resource centre at North Acton and committed itself to pay for all calls and similar expenses. It set out to motivate the hundreds of employees at North Acton to train as volunteers or help in other ways. The aim was to turn a service that operated for 12 hours a day into one running 24 hours a day, seven days a week. The company's 1000 stores were asked to put together programmes to promote the helpline number in their area. The company provided free posters and stickers with the number, and used its clout with the radio stations on which it advertised to promote the service on air. It also turned its huge annual ball for all employees into the Get Connected–CPW ball with a fundraising element.

The great thing about this partnership is that it so motivates the employees and is such a natural relationship. No one asks: why is CPW doing that?

Of course it has a huge business benefit for CPW. It promotes the company name on the posters as well as that of Get Connected. It contains the 'simple, impartial advice slogan'. It indirectly lays stress on the positive benefits of the mobile phone product. Get Connected were more than happy about that. The charity recognised that the business benefits for CPW ensured the company would feel secure about committing itself to a long-term relationship. That security is vital to any small charity. Certainly no one has criticised the partnership.

At the same time the company leadership has adopted the commitment. Chairman and Chief Executive Charles Dunstone had already been supporting Get Connected before the partnership was formed. He was fully committed. Des Wilson, who had just joined the CPW board as a non-executive director, was a former Director of Shelter and had a lifelong record of social concern. Dunstone became Chairman of Get Connected and Des Wilson joined its management board, the two bringing considerable strengths to a small charity that previously had not had the connections or experience Dunstone and Wilson could bring.

This was a classic case of 'everyone a winner': society as a whole, and its vulnerable children, who now have a well-resourced and well-marketed facility that costs the taxpayer nothing; the charity which has security and the ability to grow; and CPW which has opened up another whole promotional front in the best possible context.

Key 6: Communicate

Some companies are shy about publicising their corporate social responsibility (CSR) programmes. 'Won't it look as if we're doing it just for the credit?' they ask. Actually, if it is done properly, the answer is no. After all accountability is a key factor in CSR, so proper reporting of its programmes is a company's obligation. Stakeholders need to know that their concerns are being addressed, their interests protected. Employees need to know all that their company is doing and why, and how they can get involved. Shareholders are entitled to have the approach and the programme explained and to be helped to see the value. The community wants to know the company's response to its concerns, and to be engaged in a dialogue with the company about its activities and plans.

A MORI poll in July 2000 asked people what they felt about companies communicating their corporate citizenship activities. No less than 86 per cent said they wanted to know more about company activities. There is thus no reason to be apologetic about communicating what the company is doing; indeed, these days it is more-or-less mandatory to do so. Companies that wish to be taken seriously in this area are now expected to have their corporate social responsibility or sustainability activities independently audited and to report fully to stakeholders.

BAA began by producing local airport reports to the community, then added a corporate overview, moved on to a two-volume annual report – one part business and financial, and one part environmental and social – and finally moved to one report incorporating CSR reporting within it so as to stress its relationship with the other core aspects of the business. It puts further information on its web site.

The basic requirements for reporting are accuracy and honesty (NGOs are increasingly looking to these reports to test companies' performance alongside their rhetoric and are ready to disparage them if they make claims that cannot be substantiated), open admission of shortcomings, and independent verification.

But communication goes beyond reports, statutory or otherwise.

Having stressed that communication is primarily about accountability, we will not shrink from arguing that the company should communicate for the good business reason that it deserves and probably needs the positive image that it has earned. Heaven knows, its critics will be quick enough to condemn it when it makes a mistake or is perceived to be acting improperly. Why should it not put on record what it is doing and why?

We are not talking about boasting here. This is not a case of 'if you've got it, flaunt it'. We are talking about straightforward communication of company activity so that stakeholders know their concerns are being addressed, their views respected, their needs met.

We live with a media for whom news is usually bad news. If a company errs, that makes good copy. If it does what is right, it is 'not newsworthy'. That being the case, companies doing the right thing should not wait for the media to take notice; they should communicate what they are doing themselves.

The people have a right to know – even the good news!

Part IV

Stakeholder Companies
No Longer An Option

CHAPTER 6

Changing Companies ...
Changing World

So how much has the concept of corporate social responsibility caught on? If you ask the British public they will tell you 'not much': when faced by Mori pollsters with the proposition that 'business and commerce do not pay enough attention to their social responsibilities', 70 per cent agreed, as did 80 per cent of 'corporate social responsibility activists', 79 per cent of MPs of the governing party (Labour), and 41 per cent of business journalists (although only 15 per cent did not agree, the rest were neutral). Of course public perceptions are often out of date, and definitely are in this case, but even so the debate still raging in the business media over the validity of the concept suggests there are still those who have to be persuaded.

One of us was recently invited to present to the board of a generally progressive company the case for, and principles of, corporate citizenship, and was appalled by the lack of interest around the table. The finance director spent the whole presentation checking figures. One of the two leading directors excused himself to make a phone call. Another looked at his watch repeatedly. They did not consider the presentation seriously; instead, at best, they indulged the presenter. And yet they were hearing what we believe was a coherent, even compelling presentation directly relevant to their own business interests.

We made a presentation to the senior management team of another company and both the finance director and the director of strategy, two key players, failed to turn up, ignoring an invitation from their own chief executive. As a result of their 'leadership', their departmental managers did not come either. Everyone concerned with finance and strategy was 'too busy'. Yet these two functions were critical to the company's chance to bring about change.

We put the above experiences down to ignorance, but apathy and indifference still exist, as does a more active kind of cynicism. Leaders of even the best groups promoting corporate responsibility and sustainability talk of how it is 'hard going' to persuade some companies or senior executives that this is serious stuff. Too many still resist the concept, despite the regular flow of headlines created by companies seriously damaged by corporate irresponsibility, the influence of the increasing number of companies adopting a more progressive approach, and the impact of organisations such as Business in the Community, Tomorrow's Company, SustainAbility and Forum for the Future, all working hard to create a more enlightened business community.

Actual business behaviour, as opposed to PR rhetoric, suggests that even where the arguments are accepted in principle they are not always reflected in practice; PR 'solutions' are often preferred to real change. Despite the twenty-first century business revolution there is still environmental irresponsibility, waste of natural resources and exploitation of vulnerable communities and countries. Newspapers still report on a daily basis plant closures and redundancies as employees and often whole communities are sacrificed to pay for what have often been management mistakes.

Why is it that what seems so obvious to most of us is still difficult for some people in business to accept?

One reason is that there is still an influential group of Milton Friedman-inspired thinkers who go beyond cynicism about corporate social responsibility and actively argue a counter case. Both the UK's Social Affairs Unit and the Institute of Economic Affairs have published pamphlets attacking the idea of stakeholder companies. A column in the *Financial Times* by Martin Wolf in July 2001 acknowledged the popularity of corporate social responsibility ('To attack it is like assailing motherhood'), but continued:

> the idea is not merely undesirable but potentially dangerous. At its limits the notion of social responsibility takes the form of the triple bottom line, which corresponds to the three facets – economic, social and environmental – of that modern deity, sustainable development. Implementing the triple bottom line involves a transformation of how business operates. Shell, which has taken this idea further than most, has stated that the adoption of corporate social responsibility demands a deep shift in corporate culture, values, decision-making process and behaviour. Yet powerful objections can be made to such a radical redefinition of corporate objectives; it accepts a false critique of the market economy, it

endorses an equally mistaken view of the powers of multinational businesses; it risks spreading costly regulations world-wide; it is more likely to slow the reduction of world poverty than accelerate it; it requires companies to make highly debatable political judgements; and it threatens a form of global neo-corporatism, in which unaccountable power is shared between companies, activist groups, some organisations and a few governments.

Sceptics make four particular charges that we will seek to answer.

Charge I: Behind the pressure to adopt social responsibility lies hostility to the profit motive itself

We do not deny that a fundamental aim of a business is to make a profit for its owners. We challenge, however, the assumption that a stakeholder company is less likely to do so. On the contrary, a stakeholder approach offers for most companies the best guarantee of consistent, long-term profitability.

The phrase 'long-term' is critical here. Sceptics argue that wherever it appears that a choice has to be made between the interests of the shareholder or another stakeholder, the shareholder should prevail. But over what time scale? There may indeed be occasions when addressing the short-term interests of the customer or employee may temporarily reduce returns to the shareholder, but its hard to see how satisfying the reasonable demands and expectations of employees, and the customer in particular, can be other than in the interests of the shareholder in the longer term. The problem these days is that the thinking of many in the City has become too short term for their own good. Once more we quote BAA as a case in point: the best way to maximise BAA profits in the short term would be to stop investing £ 1 million every day on airport infrastructure, or to stop spending heavily on safety and security. But how long would the company be allowed to maintain its ownership of the nation's gateways if it failed to provide capacity or high standards of customer service, safety and security? An attempt by the Treasury in 1999–2000 to break the company up failed precisely because the company was performing well for its stakeholders. The government's inability to prove that BAA had abused its monopoly power (by putting BAA shareholders before the interests of all its other stakeholders) ensured the company's continued licence to do business in the interests of its shareholders.

Stakeholderism is about uniting all those affected directly or indirectly by the company so that together they will support its need to grow and the steps it has to take to do that. How can that ever be contrary to the interests of shareholders?

The choice these critics insist we have to make – between the shareholder and the stakeholder – is a false one. The shareholder is a stakeholder, and the enlightened shareholder understands that it is in his or her best long-term interests that the company performs for everyone who can affect the company's well-being.

As for the charge that companies adopting corporate responsibility are hostile to profit, this is demonstrably ludicrous. Would the critics really confront John Egan or Mike Hodgkinson, his successor at BAA, or John Browne at BP, or the leaders of other companies in the forefront of change, and tell them to their faces that they are 'hostile to profit'?

While we would acknowledge, as does *Built to Last*, a high quality report by the UNEP and SustainAbility, that more research is necessary, we would also accept the report's verdict that if you take the evidence as a whole 'the jury is in – overall corporate sustainable development perform-ance has a positive impact on business success'. The report's key conclusion was that 'contrary to the beliefs of Milton Friedman, sustain-ability development performance does not detract from a firm's obligation to its shareholders.... [It is] neutral at worst, and in some instances has been shown to add considerable value.'

A number of studies go further about social responsibility generally. For instance John Kettner, Professor of Leadership, and John Heskett, of the Harvard Business School, undertook a study of 200 firms in 20 sectors over four years and concluded that in 'companies with strong corporate values who effectively manage their people, turnover, earnings per share and profits increased significantly faster than the norm'.

The approach we advocate is not motivated by hostility to profit. It is motivated at least in part by a belief that sustained corporate citizenship leads to sustained profit and a sustainable company. In his book *The Living Company*, Arie de Geus looked for the common factors in companies that last: 'long lived companies'. He identified four and the first was 'long lived companies were sensitive to their environment'.

Whether they had built their fortunes on knowledge on or natural resources, they remained in harmony with the world around them.

As wars, depressions, technologies and political changes surged and ebbed around them, they always seemed to excel at keeping their feelers out, tuned to whatever was going on around them.... They managed to react in timely fashion to the conditions of society around them.

Does the search for profit in itself act as a spur to innovation and even social improvement, as the critics argue? Of course it can. But we are not arguing against a search for profit, rather that experience suggests the more sensitive the company is to the world around it, the closer it is in touch with its customers and in tune with its employees, the more it is supported by the wider community, the more likely it is that this company will be innovative, aware of the opportunities to develop, and able to profit from them. As de Geus wrote:

Behind all displays of sensitivity to the community there generally lay a hard-headed approach and a recognition that ... alertness and responsiveness ... helped create the climate in which business growth could take place.... Sensitivity to the [wider] environment represents a company's ability to learn and adapt.

The authors of *More Than Profits* found that:

contrary to business school doctrine, we did not find 'maximising shareholder wealth' or 'profit maximisation' as the dominant driving force or primary objective through the history of most visionary companies. They have tended to pursue a cluster of objectives, of which making money is only one. Indeed, for many of the visionary companies, business has historically been more than an economic activity, more than just a way to make money.... Of course we are not saying that the visionary companies have been uninterested in profitability or long-term shareholder value.... Yes they pursue profits and, yes, they pursue broader, more meaningful ideals. Profit maximisation does not rule, but the visionary companies pursue their aims profitably. They do both.

They conclude too that those companies guided by a core ideology – core values and a purpose beyond making money – 'paradoxically make more money than the more purely profit-driven comparison companies'.

This, of course, begs a question: should profit, or what is known as 'the business case', be the point anyway? Why are we bothering to argue a business case? Should companies not be ethical, socially responsible entities as a matter of principle? We could devote pages to this debate. As it happens we both strongly believe that companies are not islands unto themselves, free to set their own rules with respect to the well-being of people or the impact their behaviour has on the planet. We strongly believe that companies should not cheat or steal, bribe or corrupt, or put people or planet at risk. But we choose not to pursue that line of argument, because we also strongly believe in the strength of the business case. The fastest way to gain widespread acceptance for stakeholderism is to win the business case first, if for no other reason than it can be argued pragmatically and factually, and does not risk the appearance of sanctimony. It is true also that we prefer to prevail over our opponents on their own terms rather than take them into unfamiliar territory where it is clear that at least some of them would not be open to argument.

Let us be clear about this: it is the basis of our argument and also our experience that behaving like decent human beings and responsible citizens of our communities, cities, countries and world is not inconsistent with running a profitable business. Where these principles appear inconsistent with a company's need to make a profit, then that particular business is deeply suspect.

Furthermore, it must follow as night follows day that a company that short changes any of its stakeholders is destined to lose their sympathy and their support. There is little evidence that companies whose only concern is shareholder value out-perform the market for long.

Charge 2: The campaign for corporate social responsibility is not just anti-profit, it is anti-business

As we have noted earlier, the headline-catching protests at world leaders' conferences at Seattle, Gothenburg and Genoa reflect growing concerns about the globalisation of business and the impact this has had, in particular on poorer countries. Freer world trade and technological advances have undoubtedly led to a more global economy; we are told the number of multi-national companies has increased from 7000 to 60 000 in 30 years. The more unacceptable early manifestations of this – reflected in some of the incidents quoted in Chapter 2 where companies set up operations in poorer regions where they could exploit cheap labour with minimal regard for health or safety regulations – have helped to create a widespread feeling that globalisation is harmful. It is said that global business generally exploits the vulnerability of Third World countries, corrupts their leaders, ignores local welfare, destroys cultural diversity, imposes unfair trading terms, has no interest in local environmental protection or conservation of local resources, and, above all, is beyond accountability, with companies run by alien directors motivated solely by profit. These are serious charges and, alas, have some truth in them. However, just as industrial companies in the developed world had to change in the face of organised labour and the refusal of society to accept the worse aspects of the Industrial Revolution, so multinational companies are rapidly changing, coming to see that they too have to be accountable to the interests of their stakeholders if they are to survive. The experience of the pharmaceutical industry in South Africa, described in Chapter 2, shows that even vulnerable countries are beginning to flex their muscle with the support of world opinion. Companies will have to understand that the pressures are coming from a world that increasingly shares values across borders, both geographical and economic, and where advances in communication and education work for the citizen as well as the organisation. In the past we would not necessarily have known what an American or British company was doing to enhance its profits in a little-known corner of Africa or South America; now we do. If the world is increasingly becoming a village, so the values of the village are also becoming global.

Fortunately, while on the one hand there is rebellion against the extremes of multinational behaviour, there is on the other hand a growing realisation among many multinationals that they need to strengthen local economies if they are to create the markets of tomorrow. As Vernon Ellis, chairman of Accenture, said in a recent London lecture:

Within the next 25 years the world's population will grow by about two billion people, but most of this growth will be in the developing countries. Will these new people live in exclusion and subsistence, or will they join and expand the world's markets as new producers, consumers and investors? This is both the challenge and opportunity for global business....

Creating economic opportunity married to social goals shows how, in making the world a better place, a company makes it a better place for its own business. The process turns neglected areas into new markets and new sources of supply.... Global business is not something apart from society: its health and long-term survival depend on the global environment in which it operates.

In reply to an oft-repeated argument that 'the role of well-run companies is to make profits, not save the planet', he stingingly replies: 'I can share a secret with you: most analysts now believe that the end of the world would have a depressing effect on company profits.'

We share Vernon Ellis's view that global business has a serious case to answer. But we also share his view that it can be a big part of the solution, not the problem.

Concerns about business are not confined to multinationals. In the UK, Prime Minister Tony Blair has been in difficulty with the trade unions and activists within his own party over plans to involve the private sector in public services. Critics do not trust the private sector to put the quality of the services before their profits. By demonstrating that they are responsive to stakeholders, companies can win the trust to undertake the tasks the Prime Minister wants to assign them.

Charge 3: If companies accept excessively costly operating practices, they are likely to be less competitive and less profitable, and so contribute less to the economy

The issue here is simple: what is the true cost of a product or service? We believe it is the traditional cost of manufacture and/or provision plus the cost of meeting the minimal standards that society as a whole would like to impose upon the products and services it subscribes to. These minimal standards require that the products are healthy and safe and will not endanger life or limb in the present, and that they are not destructive to our children and our children's children by polluting the planet or squandering non-renewable resources without providing alternatives. Put this in the context of BAA: we believe the cost of aviation should not only include the basic cost of manufacturing aircraft, administering and promoting airlines, and operating airports, but also unimpeachable standards of health and safety, the unending pursuit of technological advance in clean engine technology, energy conservation and reductions in noise, and the provision of high-quality public transport to and from cities. All of this is about sustainability and should underpin the right to grow. And, yes, the industry as a whole and its customers should pay the price. That is what Mike Hodgkinson has been arguing in his ground-breaking speeches to industry conferences; that is what Contract with the Community programme and the sustainability programme are all about, in so much as BAA alone can make a difference.

Does a stakeholder approach automatically mean a negative effect on the bottom line? We have already suggested it does not. The positive case is convincing and does not rely on particular savings to be made in specific instances, though there are many that could be cited. For example, it is clear that energy conservation cuts energy bills (fuel is the number one cost of an airline; who has a greater need to conserve energy?); high standards of safety and security mean companies do not have to compensate – let alone explain away – the injured; corporate citizenship enhances the reputation and goodwill towards the brand; good employee practices mean retaining and achieving greater productivity from your best employees; and improved customer care means satisfied customers who often spend more, and come back more often.

Charge 4: Judgements of what these concepts mean are political. Are business people the right people to make those judgements? If so, how and by what authority do they do so?

Frankly this is a nonsense. Any sixth former could today spell out to you the fundamental meaning of corporate social responsibility or citizenship, of stakeholderism and sustainability. And any sixth former would understand that this is not driven by a 'political' agenda but by the shared values of a community that has no difficulty reaching a view about what is and is not just, or what is or is not right. It is only when organisations assume a kind of institutional mindset that allows no room for human values that these things are not understood.

Ironically, the economic right-wingers here find themselves on the same side as the globalisation protesters, the latter believing that democratic institutions rather than business should set the standards and write the codes of conduct. Maybe when it is a matter of detailed articles of environmental protection this may be so, but the human race has never needed legislators to tell it what is right and what is wrong, just a conscience. Most of the issues that have led to protests about the behaviour of global business are not complicated; they are about basic human rights, decent treatment of workers and concern for human safety; and companies know what to do because they are already doing it in Western countries.

We have already considered activist groups. Suffice it to say that they are part of the democratic process, not a challenge to it, and how much or how little influence they have depends on whether they reflect the needs and views of society as a whole. Des Wilson, who has been heavily involved in activist groups in the past, says he knows of no case where activist groups have won where they were not working with the grain of public opinion or able to identify their specific cause with more widely held public views.

Rather than subverting individual freedom, most activist groups are made up of individuals exercising their freedom; rather than subverting democracy, they enhance it by provoking debate and highlighting issues that otherwise would be obscured. But at the end of the day they have no power but the power to persuade.

Having addressed these issues, how can we move business and industry on in this area? First, by drawing in the new generation. Clearly business schools need to bring corporate citizenship and sustainability to the fore-front of their syllabus. We need a new breed of young business people, not only educated to succeed in today's tough, competitive, highly technolog-ical, international business world, but also educated as citizens of the world, with wider perspectives and an understanding of how profitable business and corporate citizenship go hand in hand.

The corporate citizenship case needs more advocates, more leaders. 'Campaigning' organisations in this area need to recruit more influential business leaders who will gain the attention of their peers, and need to be more forceful and imaginative in promoting the cause. Business organisa-tions need to embrace the case and lead the charge. Investors, who have much to gain from the business benefits of corporate citizenship, should also bring their influence to bear.

We believe the public relations/public affairs profession, so sensitive to its appalling image, could do much to improve its standing and be taken more seriously if it got off its knees, became less sycophantic and oppor-tunistic, and took on the company advocate role described by Des Wilson in this book; it has the potential, if it properly represents the interests of stakeholders to its clients or employers, to be far more influential. To quote US journalist Sam Smith once more, 'the best public relations is to do the right thing'.

Fundamentally, this is about vision and leadership, and that means the men and women at the top listening carefully to the concerns and views of their stakeholders, and leading their colleagues to respond.

What are the key messages we have to get across to those who remain cynical or just plain indifferent?

Perhaps the first, and we state this unashamedly, is that this is about good business. It is not a threat to the bottom line, it is essential to it. The whole shareholder versus stakeholder debate has always been a false one; now it borders on the ludicrous. We repeat the argument we have already made: how can a shareholder feel secure if his business is under assault or being rejected by customers, or its own employees, or by the local community, or any other interested group. How can a business grow if planning committees and other influential bodies are only too ready to refuse it permission? How can it have a competitive edge if its competitors have greater reputation and goodwill?

The second message is that this is not about PR. It is about the values of the company, the kind of people in it, the kind of ethical and other beliefs at its core. A company that loves its work and loves the people it works with will prosper; a company that does not care will fail.

The third is that the evidence is now convincing: 'good' companies prosper; 'bad' ones pay a heavy price. How many major companies must face embarrassing headlines, demonstrations, AGM protests, customer boycotts, governmental disapproval and regulatory action before others understand that if they are to avoid the same fate they should do what is right?

The fourth message is that we are still at a starting point in this process: the twenty-first century revolution still has a long way to go. Industry as a whole and each company in particular – this of course, includes BAA, whose case history is at the heart of this book – are launched on an exciting journey; objectives are being radically re-focused; the values of communities and corporations have to be brought together to the mutual benefit of both; radically improved and inclusive relationships with stakeholders must be attained; ways of working are beginning to be radically changed.

The entire business community needs to embrace the change. All reasonable people should encourage it, and that means enthusing about positive change as well as complaining about the bad, and working with this grain rather than allowing cynicism and impatience to impede improvement.

We wrote this book because we believe these related concepts of corporate citizenship and responsibility, sustainability, and stakeholderism are ones that need to be central to any twenty-first century company that hopes to grow, expand and live in harmony with neighbours and other stakeholders, retain the loyalty and pride of its employees, and ultimately deliver for its shareholders.

We wrote it because we think not enough attention is being paid to the positive change that has been happening, to the twenty-first century revolution. We stress one more time that in our discussion of BAA we do not claim that the company has yet got it all right. While we were working for it, however, we both became convinced about its need to be a stakeholder company, we learned our lessons, and, thanks to the enthusiasm and actions of our colleagues who are now carrying on the work, we have seen real results for community and company alike.

We urge everyone in business and industry to adopt these concepts.

The future of their companies and their industries, the case for economic growth and the harmony of our world may depend on it.

Appendices

The Centre for Tomorrow's Company

The Centre for Tomorrow's Company (CTC) seeks to provide a focal point for those pursuing enduring business excellence. It is a business-led, not-for-profit think-tank and catalyst, researching and stimulating a new agenda for business. The focus of its work is upon the issues of business leadership and governance.

Simply put, Tomorrow's Company is a vision of business that makes equal sense to shareholders and society alike. It believes a business that ignores social values will not deliver lasting returns. An economy that ignores them will not be worth living in. CTC summarises these values as an inclusive approach that places leadership and relationships at the heart of success

Its research programmes are currently focusing on the future of the investment industry, an examination of what makes for a successful company and the link between company values and the global economy.

Published in June 2001, CTC's first report on the future of investment, *Twenty-first Century Investment: An Agenda for Change*, was commended by the CBI, ProShare, SustainAbility and leading figures in the investment field. This work continues with current projects exploring how the different parties in the investment decision-making chain can bridge the gap between consumer expectations and pension industry practice.

To keep its thinking fresh and its practical applications relevant, CTC continues to investigate what makes for durable corporate success. Its work in this area is currently concerned with leadership and employee-owned companies, and it is collecting case studies where corporate value has been built by taking an inclusive approach.

Initial work around values and globalisation has been promising, with a significant number of UK-based trans-nationals becoming involved in discussing the challenges of ethical codes in a global setting. Further projects in this programme are planned.

Membership of the Centre for Tomorrow's Company is available at three levels to suit the needs and pockets of different groups and individuals. All members gain access to our research papers, practical tools, publications and events, although benefits are pegged to the level of membership fees.

As with all membership organisations, CTC depends on the generosity of its members to promote its work and thereby improve the membership experience. It encourages those organisations that can to donate over and above its outline tariffs. Where appropriate, additional donations may be made in kind.

CTC's members are drawn from across business. They include the Department of Trade and Industry, John Lewis Partnership, Land Securities, Royal & Sun Alliance, Shell and Unipart.

For more information on CTC or our work please see its website: www.tomorrowscompany.com

Mark Goyder
The Centre for Tomorrow's Company
19 Buckingham Street
London
WC2N 6EF
Telephone 020 7930 5150
Fax 020 7930 5155
info@tomorrowscompany.com

APPENDIX 2

SustainAbility

'Constructive discomfort' was the way one major energy sector client summed up a key part of SustainAbility's value added for his company. Founded in 1987 and now based in London and New York, Sustain-Ability specialises in business strategy and sustainable development (SD). The organisation was a hybrid from the outset: part award-winning consultancy, part world-class think-tank, part energetic public interest group. SustainAbility is for-profit, but not primarily profit-driven.

Leaders in triple bottom line (TBL) research and advice, SustainAbility focuses attention on the economic, social and environmental value added – or destroyed – by a product, value chain, company or industry sector.

The organisation has three main focus areas: foresight, agenda-setting and change management. A core team of 20 people, of 10 nationalities, is advised by an independent Council of 10 and a faculty of over 50 experts from 12 countries. SustainAbility is certified by Climate Care and by Investors in People (IiP).

On the consultancy side, the work is a mixture of one-off projects and longer-term relationships, mainly with companies. The services offered range from stakeholder engagement and report benchmarking through to SD reviews and boardroom counsel. Clients include Aventis, the Ford Motor Company, Holcim, ING, the International Finance Corporation, Nike, Novartis, Novo Nordisk, Philips and Shell.

In terms of foresight and though leadership, a series of SustainAbility books and reports have laid out the TBL agenda for business. In the early years, such books as *The Green Capitalists* (1987) and *The Green Consumer Guide* (a number one bestseller in 1988) helped spur corporate innovation. More recent books have explored the sustainability agenda for business: *Cannibals With Forks: The Triple Bottom Line of Twenty-First Century Business* (1997) and *The Chrysalis Economy: How Citizen CEOs and Corporations Can Fuse Values and Value Creation* (2001).

In parallel, a series of research programmes have produced a series of agenda-shaping reports. The longest-running programme, in partnership with the United Nations Environment Programme (UNEP) and sponsored by over 20 major companies, is 'Engaging Stakeholders'. Launched in 1993, this has produced more than a dozen reports, the latest of which focus on best practice in corporate sustainability reporting (*The Global Reporters*, 2001) and in auto sector reporting (*Driving Sustainability*, 2001).

Among the more recently launched research programmes, one (with the IBLF) focuses on corporate governance and the role of boards, a second (with the UN) on the business case for sustainable development, and a third (with GPC) on best practice in corporate public policy positioning. Further information is available from: www.sustainability.com.

Forum for the Future

The Forum's mission is to accelerate the building of a sustainable way of life, taking a positive, solutions-oriented approach.

Forum for the Future was founded in 1996 by three of the UK's leading advocates of sustainable development: Jonathon Porritt, Sara Parkin and Paul Ekins. They did so out of a conviction that many of the solutions needed to defuse the environmental crisis, and to build a more sustainable society, are already to hand.

These economic, social and technological solutions can deliver not just a healthy environment, but a better quality of life, strong communities, and practical answers to poverty and disempowerment.

Forum for the Future is playing a unique role in bringing people together to work out these solutions, and apply them in practice. The Forum works at a strategic level through its partnerships to maximise its impact.

The Forum is a small organisation, based in London and Cheltenham. With around 60 core and project staff, we will never measure our success by turnover or staff numbers. But, with our partners, we can wield influence where it's most needed: among decision makers and opinion formers.

The Forum channels its work through a range of main activities: a mix of consultancy, research, advocacy, education, media provision, and capacity building in the business, government and higher education sectors. The core programmes within the Forum provide a complete and integrated solution to sustainability issues in the sectors outlined above. By pursuing partnerships with key organisations, the Forum has developed several cutting-edge initiatives that are pushing forward the sustainability agenda in the UK.

In the work we do, the Forum is playing a vital role in shifting the environmental agenda beyond stale confrontation into positive, dynamic partnerships for lasting change. Our definition of sustainable development is: 'A dynamic process which enables all people to realise their potential and to improve their quality of life in ways which simultaneously protect and enhance the Earth's life support systems'. Forum programmes directed toward this end include:

- The Sustainable Economy Programme: policy-oriented economic solutions to environmental problems.
- The Education and Learning Programme: partnerships in higher education and the Forum's own Scholarship Programme.
- The Natural Step: a science-based training initiative for business and other sectors, developed in Sweden and introduced to the UK by the Forum.
- Forum Directory of Sustainability in Practice: providing decision-makers with easy access to cutting-edge practice in sustainable development.
- *Green Futures*: the UK's leading bi-monthly magazine communicating examples of environmental solutions and sustainable futures.
- Forum Local and Regional Programme: working with key players in the regions and in local authorities to implement sustainable development.
- Forum Business Programme: helping companies map a route through the rapidly evolving sustainable development agenda.

For further information visit the website:
    www.forumforthefuture.org.uk
or e-mail inquiries to:
    info@forumforthefuture.org.uk

Business in the Community

Business in the Community (BITC) is a unique movement of companies across the UK committed to continually improving their positive impact on society, with a core membership of 700 companies, including 70 per cent of the FTSE 100. Members of BITC are committed to:

- Developing business excellence: continually improving, measuring and reporting the impact their business has on their environment, workplace, marketplace and community.
- Developing community excellence: actively engaging in partnerships to tackle disadvantage and create enterprising communities.

Since its creation in 1982, BITC has championed socially responsible business practices; since 1985 it has operated as a business-led organisation, under the hands-on presidency of HRH The Prince of Wales. It initiated the International Business Leaders Forum in 1990 and also now works closely with partner organisations in CSR Europe and internationally. The prestigious annual BITC Awards for Excellence have become the premier awards of their kind.

Individual BITC campaigns champion corporate innovation in areas such as Business in the Environment, cause-related marketing, employee volunteering and business action on homelessness.

e-mail: information@bitc.org.uk
www.bitc.org.uk
www.business-impact.org

Index